Dear Jalisa,

To women s[...]

Love, Monica

monicabennett.net

# HOW MAY I SERVE

MEMOIRS FROM A SPIRITUAL WAITRESS

KAREN MATHEWS

BALBOA.
PRESS

A DIVISION OF HAY HOUSE

Balboa Press books may be ordered through booksellers or by contacting:

Balboa Press
A Division of Hay House
1663 Liberty Drive
Bloomington, IN 47403
www.balboapress.com
1 (877) 407-4847

Because of the dynamic nature of the Internet, any web addresses or
links contained in this book may have changed since publication and
may no longer be valid. The views expressed in this work are solely those
of the author and do not necessarily reflect the views of the publisher,
and the publisher hereby disclaims any responsibility for them.

The author of this book does not dispense medical advice or prescribe the use
of any technique as a form of treatment for physical, emotional, or medical
problems without the advice of a physician, either directly or indirectly. The
intent of the author is only to offer information of a general nature to help
you in your quest for emotional and spiritual well-being. In the event you use
any of the information in this book for yourself, which is your constitutional
right, the author and the publisher assume no responsibility for your actions.

Any people depicted in stock imagery provided by Thinkstock are models,
and such images are being used for illustrative purposes only.
Certain stock imagery © Thinkstock.

Printed in the United States of America.

ISBN: 978-1-4525-1523-6 (sc)
ISBN: 978-1-4525-1525-0 (hc)
ISBN: 978-1-4525-1524-3 (e)

Library of Congress Control Number: 2014909108

Balboa Press rev. date: 06/09/2014

# CHAPTER 1

E very morning, right after waking up, I would ask God, "How may I serve? How may I be of service to my highest good?"

And every night, just before I went to sleep, again I would ask God for guidance: "How may I be of service? How may I serve to my highest calling?"

I just never thought God would take me literally. I asked to be of service ... and now I am a server again. A waitress? Really?

Now I am serving many people, all day; however, I am not so sure that this is my highest calling. I have so much to give; so much I desire to offer. I have so much knowledge, wisdom, inspiration, and motivation that I want to bring forth. I feel like I am trapped between two worlds, one being a "light worker"—someone who is helping to heal the planet and is ready, willing, and able to assist in transmuting the world to a higher frequency—and the other in this dense, dark, old carbon-based world, dragging me down back into my reptilian brain.

I get up at 4:20 each morning. I feed my four cats, wash, get dressed, meditate for fifteen minutes, and then walk my cute little ten-pound, long-haired Chihuahua. I give him a treat, make my bed, and off I go at 5:30AM to work. I live on Long Island, and it takes me about twenty minutes to get to work.

I start my shift at 6:00AM and always get there a bit early. I like my habits. I like being punctual, and I like being organized. I have learned, and still believe, that being late is a sign of disrespect. My shift is from 6:00 in the morning to 3:00 in the afternoon, Thursday through Monday. My weekends are Tuesdays and Wednesdays. My work shifts are long, with most of the time being spent on my feet.

I am a morning person, so I really enjoy this time of day the most. It is quiet and magical. I can think of many other things I could do with my mornings rather than head off to the Mystic Luncheonette, but this is where I am called to be at the moment. This is where I am serving and giving what is needed of me to raise the consciousness of people's lives as well as my own. This is my ministry for now. There are lessons to be learned here too.

I do sometimes get to spread my light-working wings, but so much of my passion is sucked from me by the energy vampires who only want their eggs cooked just right and their toast dry.

Yuck! I don't sound very spiritual, do I?

———~m·o·ᴐⅇᴛⱺ⑄ⅇ·o·m———

Being a waitress is truly a study in psychology. Anyone who wants to go into psychology needs to be a server to some degree. You really get a full spectrum of human behavior when you serve food to people. To be a good server, you need to have people skills, ask lots of questions, be quick on your feet, be able to multitask, have a good memory, balance well, and smile at all times.

Food is such an emotional issue for so many people, and at a luncheonette in a small community, you get to see a lot of the same people day in and day out. They sit at the same table, (if it is available). They order the same thing day after day, only switching it up on weekends, and they like to be served in the same way, by the same server. We are all creatures of habit.

The Mystic Luncheonette on Long Island, New York has quite the history. It has been around since 1932, so you can just imagine the array of people who have passed through these doors. I believe places hold energy. When you walk into a beautiful church or any house of worship, you can feel the calm, peaceful aura in the space it holds. The Mystic Luncheonette also is holding the energy of all the people who have come and gone before. It is very active and highly unpredictable.

Working here as a server, I sometimes feel that I am also locked into a paradigm that is in desperate need of change. I see the world, our Earth, crying out for help. I see people manifesting disease in their bodies and minds, rather than ease and peace. How can I serve better? How can I be of help? How can I use my skills and talents to wake them up from the nightmare they are in?

Before working at the luncheonette, I had a successful horticulture business for twenty-three years. I worked for the crème de la crème of clients. I have a degree in natural health. I am a certified reflexologist and life coach. I developed an aromatherapy body spray, made to balance your chakras, called Hygiea, after the goddess of health. That is where we get the word *hygiene,* and where all health began. I am a biodynamic gardener and an amazing dancer. I studied with the best teachers in the world in personal development and spent tens of thousands of dollars on my education. I have traveled the world and experienced more than most people do in a lifetime.

So being a waitress really threw me for a loop. I don't believe in accidents, so I know I am here for a reason and that there is purpose lurking here somewhere. The key is to discover this reason.

I want to scream from the rooftops that it is time to think differently, to live differently. But sadly, no one hears me; no one is interested.

Oh, yes, there are a few lonely souls like me out there with whom I can converse, but most people just want their pancakes, french toast, eggs, and burgers. They want comfort, routine, and habits. They don't want change, and they certainly don't want to shake their lives up; unless, of course, it comes in chocolate.

I love people, and I love to help and teach the laws of nature and of the universe. I am fascinated by metaphysical phenomena, healing, energy, consciousness, nature, the mind, and the capacity we have to explore the infinite possibilities that we can tap into when we make the quantum shifts within ourselves, those minute changes that will alter our lives in a big way.

Is *that* how I am here being a server again? Is that why I wound up at the Mystic Luncheonette, waitressing at fifty-six years young?

Let's see. Let's go back in time … way, way back, before I was even a twinkle in my parents' eyes, to discover how I ended up here, shall we?

# CHAPTER 2

Both of my parents were from Germany. My father was born in Berlin in 1926 to extremely wealthy Jewish parents. My mother was born in Munich in 1929 to a lower-income but educated family. Her mom was Catholic and her father was Jewish. They never married because of this. There was already unrest in Germany at this time, and marriage was not advisable. So Mom was an illegitimate child, which was also frowned upon. Neither of my parents had siblings, so I have no aunts, uncles, or cousins. My dad's life was full of nannies, servants, expensive clothing, Rolls-Royce automobiles, and all the other finer things in life. From the stories I am told, his dad was the jovial one. I was told my grandfather spent more time with my dad than my grandmother did, and from the pictures that I still have, you can see that this was the case.

I never saw pictures of my grandmother with my father; only my grandfather and the nannies are posed with him. I never did get to meet my grandfather, so I have to recount all of this only from the stories that were told to me. He was a womanizer and loved playing the horses. This did not sit well with his wife, my grandmother. She was very proper and snooty. They had friends in all the right places (including some high Nazi officials) and connections to get what they needed and wanted.

My grandmother, whom I did know, was a real bitch, I'm sorry to say. She was very cold. (I know that doesn't sound too spiritual, but hey, who says being spiritual and having a potty-mouth can't go hand-in-hand?) From the tales I was told, she was off skiing, gallivanting at parties, and doing what she wanted while my dad was left with the nannies and servants. Again, I have pictures that back up this scenario, so it must be at least somewhat close to the truth. It was their lifestyle, for a while at least.

Then the shit hit the fan. The war broke out. Chaos, unrest, hiding, bombs, and uncertainty all came to play in my parents' lives. My dad had to see his father off on the trains, heading toward a concentration camp. I'm sure my dad wasn't told his father was going there, but it was a cattle car, so it must have been awful. I can't even fathom what my dad or my grandfather was experiencing and feeling.

I was told that my grandfather could have been spared. He might have been able to leave Germany, since they had connections with high officials; however, my grandmother did not want this to happen because of his flirtatious nature. She could have saved his life; instead she let him die. Horrible, simply horrible.

My dad was able to get out. He was sent to London, England, the only country accepting German-Jewish children. When he arrived, there were families ready to adopt children into their homes. They only wanted the very young children, though, since they felt that they would be easier to handle. My dad, being a bit older—around sixteen—was not taken in by any family, so he wound up living in several orphanages and working in factories. When I think of what he had to go through, my heart bleeds for him. What a sad story. My grandmother eventually paid her way out to London. Everything was taken from them by the Nazis. Their home, belongings, bank accounts—anything of value. To this day, all that I have from my grandmother is a diamond ring and some pictures that she was able to smuggle out. My grandfather, well, we found no record of him ever arriving at any concentration camp. So we had to assume he must have died on the train and they just threw him out. The whole story is just awful.

———— ⚬⚬⚬ ————

My mother lived in an apartment building in the center of Munich with her mom, and her grandparents, who lived nearby. She, being half Jewish, was considered just as "bad" as being fully Jewish. My mom always felt alone and unloved. My grandmother had her at a young age, and she never had the patience to care for her in a nurturing way. Besides, with everything that was going on in Germany at this time, my grandmother felt it difficult to express her feelings in a healthy way. It was a tough time for everyone, and my grandmother had a lot of suppressed anger, guilt, and shame— both about having a child out of wedlock and having conceived a child from a man who was Jewish. My grandfather was a Sephardic Jew, born in Amsterdam, Holland. He was a chemist and a gifted horticulturist. (I sometimes wonder if somehow his spirit surrounds me, since I have the same gift.) He loved people and loved to engage in conversation about philosophy, nature, and life. He did not live with my mom and grandmother, and I'm not sure how he got to Munich or how he met my grandmother. I do know that my mom had major abandonment issues due to the fact that she was an illegitimate child and half Jewish. Many things were kept hidden from her to protect her from the Nazis, which she didn't understand. This caused her to develop phobias and insecurities that have remained with her to this day. As a child she was often in hiding from the third Reich since her birth certificate showed that she was half Jewish. This was tremendously stressful for her and my grandmother, who was trying to protect her from being taken away.

She was sent to school, but never wanted to go out of fear that something would happen to her mom and grandparents. Nothing and nowhere was safe. At home, there was always the chance of an unexpected interrogation by the Nazis. There were air raids and bomb attacks daily. Once, while at school, the air raids sounded off and all the children were told to go into the shelters at the school. My mom recounts that instead of hiding, she ran home, bombs going off all around her. She didn't care; she just wanted to get home to her family. The next day, she told me that she saw the devastation all around, and that her school was gone. Her intuition must have been very powerful to have told her to run home instead of stay there. She would have been killed.

After the bombing at her school, my mom was sent to another school. My grandmother had studied dressmaking and so she pushed my mom to do the same. She has an amazing talent for it—she is very artistic. I still have some pieces of clothing in excellent condition that are so detailed that any designer would be envious of the workmanship that went into them. At this time, my grandfather was sent to a place in the country where he could hide and have protection from the Nazis. Unfortunately, he died of malnutrition and loneliness. They couldn't get food to him and no one came to visit because it was too dangerous. I wish I'd been able to meet my grandfathers.

———————

My maternal grandmother had one sister and three brothers. I was fortunate to have gotten to know my great aunt, Tante Annie (in German, Tante means aunt) and Onkel Oscar (in German, Onkel means uncle). Oscar was an engineer. I never did get to meet the two other brothers. Onkel Irving was studying to become a doctor and in order to complete his thesis, he had to go to the front lines in battle; it was there that he was killed by shrapnel. When my great grandmother received the news of his death, it killed her. She had a heart attack that she never recovered from.

Before her death, she was a brave woman during the war. I was told that she took many people into her house that were in hiding and couldn't find work. They had a carpenter, a strip teaser, and many others, such as Gypsies and Jews who would have been sent off to concentration camps if it weren't for my great grandmother. It really is amazing how one's true character is revealed during times of crisis and stress. Looking back, I admire her strength, courage, and open heart, and I often feel her presence around me. I'm not too sure what happened to the other brother, Onkel Hans. He had a few children, I was told, but I never knew or had any contact with them. Between my father's story of tragedy, and my mother's story of despair, it really is a miracle they were able to find each other.

# CHAPTER 3

The war went on and on until one day it was over. The bloodshed stopped, the bombs were muted, the concentration camps were liberated, and the damage was done—which continues from generation to generation until we learn to live in peace with one another.

Now my parents were young adults. They should have been exploring their freedom and having fun. While things were better for them after the war; however, they both had deep psychological scars that would have lasting effects. My father, at this time, was working as a civilian for the American forces and was transferred to Hamburg, Germany. It was there that he met Francis Koch, a businessman who owned a few small women's retail shops in Munich. They became very close friends and he asked my father if he would like to go to Munich with him. He did, and that is where he met my mother. Ah, so romantic. An after-war love story. They were both, by chance, invited to go out to dinner one evening. Sometimes you have to wonder about these chance meetings. I don't believe in chance or luck; I believe in divine intervention. After all, these two war-torn people, whose lives could have been over any number of times, wound up at the same place at the same time. I believe that when you are really ready for something to show up in your life, the forces of nature collaborate to make it happen. Well, whether they were ready or not, the great law of attraction was pulling them together like a magnet.

There is a term called "SyncroDestiny," coined by Deepak Chopra, which means a combination of synchronicity and destiny. I think my parents' meeting was most definitely SyncroDestiny. My dad was smitten by my mother's beauty and innocence. She was all of twenty years old and my father twenty-three. I'm sure there were major flirtatious exchanges taking place. I wish I could have been a fly on the wall, observing them. He asked if he could take her out on a date. My mom, who was shy, said that he would have to ask her mother first to see if she approved. Can you even imagine that happening today? Anyway, he did. He brought my grandmother flowers—what a gentleman. So they became a couple. Even though they were young and didn't have much in common, I think the war bonded them. They were both German, but my father was very proper and refined in manner. The Northern Germans are considered to be Hochdeutsch or upper German. My mom, who comes from Munich (Southern Germany) was Bayerisch, or more countrified. They were young, in love, and desperate for a new life. They did not stay in Munich long before they decided to get married and head for America, the Promised Land. There was no big fancy wedding with a beautiful dress and a big party. It was only a small, intimate ritual with my grandmother and some other relatives present. Off they were, onto a ship headed to Ellis Island and America, home of the free and land of the brave. Their new life awaited them, and they began to discover a place of endless opportunity.

I am always awed by the stories of people who left everything behind and ventured to a foreign land with little, if any, resources. You don't speak the language, you don't have a job, you have a little money and a few contacts. However, out of nothing you create something. Isn't that how everything came about, anyway?

Everything is created twice, once in the mind and then in physical form. We must think it before it can be manifested. Actually, when coming from nothing, you can start fresh and create anything if you're open to the infinite possibilities of life. You just have to leave the baggage of your past behind to make room for the new to come in. Yes, this is what my parents did. They stepped into their next experience. Unfortunately, they did have quite a bit of baggage, which wasn't unpacked for years to come.

---

While my father was in Hamburg, he made friends with an American soldier by the name of Martin Lenstein. He was a German-Jew who came to America with his family before the war broke out, and as a young man he went back to Germany as an American soldier. Martin was very confident, outgoing, and witty. He had a charm about him that attracted people to him. There was a rough edge to him, too. If someone provoked him, they'd be best to watch out. While both in America, my father and Martin soon became good friends. While Martin was a soldier he met a Russian girl by the name of Nadia, who was working as a nanny for a Nazi family during the war.

Nadia, dear Nadia. I have fond memories and happy thoughts when I think of her. Nadia had a fascinating war story. She was born in to a Russian Orthodox family on the Eastern side of the Baltic Sea, and although I really didn't know too much about her life back in Russia, I picture Nadia being a strong, happy, determined girl. Her laugh was contagious and I could see her eyes sparkle with life. She told me that she would often sneak away from home and wander off for days. She was a real free spirit and adventurer. Their family was of the lower class and didn't have very much; but their basic needs were always met—until the war broke out. Then there was no food. No shipment of any kind was allowed to come into Russia. The people were cold, hungry, and desperate. She would tell me that they would pick the bugs out of the soil to eat. They survived on the most basic of essentials and somehow, by the grace of God and sheer willpower, they managed to persevere.

During these chaotic times, the family somehow became divided. The Germans came in to Russia looking for workers to bring back to Germany. Nadia and some other young girls had an opportunity to leave Russia, so they did. She traveled by train, arriving weeks later somewhere in Southern Germany. Just imagine an eighteen-year-old woman alone, off to an unknown destination and a future completely left to faith. I'm not sure if I would have been so brave. I believe because of her strong nature, she was able to endure all the hardships with a calm spirit, even if her body was trembling with fear. She traveled for days on rations meant for mice. Exhausted, hungry, and dirty, she finally arrived in Bavaria. This would be her new home for the next few years. The Nazis herded all the girls off the train and corralled them like slaves in a circle. When they were all together, a German official yelled out, "Who knows how to speak German?" She didn't understand what he was saying, but she saw other girls raise their hands, so she felt compelled to do so also. Nadia went on to work for a high-ranking Nazi family of the Third Reich. She was to become a housekeeper and a nanny for five children.

Her new home was opulent but cold. There were riches and abundance everywhere she turned; however, she had no access to any of it. Nadia would have to live in a small room the size of a broom closet and only come out to do her work. She learned the basics of the German language, and was a quick learner in other ways too, since she often got lashes from the Mrs. of the house if anything was not to her liking.

Nadia had some of her most lonely years there. No playtime, no music, no fun; none of the things the average American teenager would be doing. No, Nadia was confined to a life of slavery. This German family practically owned her, and years went by as she endured this torturous existence. She did get to have some free time once in a while and go into town to mingle with other workers; it was there that she met Martin. Martin, being the charming, charismatic man that he was, attracted Nadia immediately. They developed a courtship, which gave Nadia hope for the future. Eventually, all bad things had come to an end for Nadia; she was liberated and free. Martin and Nadia were soon off to America.

My father and Martin had devised a plan to meet up once they'd both arrived in the States, since my father didn't have any other connections. These were new beginnings, a fresh start, and infinite possibilities. The world was open to them; at least it seemed that way. My parents had very little money, a few suitcases, and a few dreams. Most of their aspirations were suppressed however, as fear tends to have a paralyzing effect on the psyche. But life did get better and there were some good times. They set up house in Newark, New Jersey, next to Nadia and Martin apartment. My mom quickly became best friends with Nadia, as my dad was best friends with Martin. My mom could not have been more different than Nadia, as if they had been picked out from two different universes. Nadia was outgoing, gregarious, and always smiling, while my mom was shy, serious, and more studious. They were somehow a good balance for one another, sort of like the yin and yang of friendship.

Nadia was like a second mother to me. She was strong, both emotionally and physically. I know so many of my behaviors are the result of these two women's influence on my life. They were both hard workers; a trait that I inherited as well. It wasn't until later that I realized I didn't always have to work so hard *physically,* and that I could better contribute to the world with meaningful and powerful work that sustains my energy.

———⁓⁓⁓⁓⁓⁓———

It was in Newark, New Jersey, where my brother Michael, Steven (Nadia and Martin's only child), and I were born. My brother was the first to arrive on this planet, in 1953. Nadia recounts a story about how excited she was about seeing the baby when my mom was ready to give birth. After the baby came, Nadia rushed to the hospital. She looked at all the babies through the window, saw Michael, and almost fainted. She said she had never seen an uglier baby—that he looked like my father's mother. When Nadia told us that story, we laughed hysterically. In the pictures, my brother was all shriveled up. He looked like an old man, although I thought he looked adorable. Luckily for him, he grew up to be a very handsome man.

Nadia was more nurturing than my mother was; She had to teach my mom how to diaper and nurse Michael. My mom had no clue how to even hold a baby, care for one, or cuddle with one. How could she? She was still a child herself. She never did mentally grow up. The doctors, at first, were going to diagnose Michael with Autism (even back then they were beginning to label children) because he did not speak until about three years of age. It turns out that he has an exceptionally high IQ, and is now a member of MENSA. He is extremely bright, especially in mathematics and languages. He is able to use both the right and the left hemispheres of his brain for a holistic view.

Steven, Nadia and Martin's son, was born one year later at the same hospital in Newark. Nadia had some complications giving birth, and she never was able to conceive another child. I believe she would have liked to have another baby. My mom, dad,

15

Martin, and Nadia were all working hard at the time, saving their money to buy houses and move outside the city to the suburbs, where there was more room to grow. Though they were working hard, they were also having a good time. There were lots of parties, gaiety, and celebrations that took place.

Three years later, my mom became pregnant again, with me. My father did not want another child and told my mom to get an abortion. I wonder if the fetus that I was at the time had any cellular consciousness of this fact. After all, we know now that a baby within the womb responds to the emotions, vibrations, and stimuli of the parents' energy. Abortions were illegal then, and to find a legitimate doctor who would perform this procedure was not easy. There were charlatans who would do it for a price, which could include your life. Many women bled to death from the hands of these butchers. Nadia told me that my mom would try to miscarriage me. She would purposefully fall down a flight of steps, or sit on the washing machine and let it jiggle and jolt her in the hopes of my dying from all the shaking. Perhaps it is the reason I am now such a great dancer. I showed them they couldn't get rid of me that easily—I wanted to live!

My journey to always seek the truth and look for the answers of who we really are as spiritual beings having this human experience was etched into the core of my being. As my mother's pregnancy progressed, my father was not too pleased about me still being around. He wanted to travel, see the world, explore. My brother was very well behaved, so one child was just right for him. Two would complicate his life, which I most certainly did. Now he began to tell my mom that when I was born she needed to find a suitable family that would adopt me. They met with several families to interview them to see if they could provide a decent home for me. I wonder who, what, and where I would have been if I had been adopted into another family. Maybe in an alternate universe I am a professional dancer or a doctor. Maybe a waitress, too! Oh no, not that. Maybe I am all of these at once, here in this world.

My mom just couldn't go through with it. This is one of the only times I believe she actually stood up for herself with my dad, or anyone else for that matter. So I was born on November 11, 1956, to Susan and George Mathews. My father had changed his name when he arrived in the States. His birth name was Hans Gunther Israel—can you tell he was a German Jew? I am an Israelite, a seeker of God. I have come back to my roots. I know my father had no awareness of his amazing ancestry. He denounced the Jewish religion and changed his name because he lived in fear of being persecuted again. My mom's maiden name was Lisa Anna Breiss. My father did not like Lisa Anna because it sounded too German, so she became Susan. I have no idea why he picked Susan.

So out I came. Thank God I was cute. If I looked like my brother, all shriveled up, I surely would have been left on someone's doorstep.

My parents decided to keep me. My father softened, and he embraced my tiny little soul into his heart.

# CHAPTER 4

By the time I was born, life was getting ever more complicated and speeding up very quickly. Martin and Nadia bought a machine shop business and a house in New Jersey. They were working hard and it was paying off. Their business was growing and money was coming in.

My father and mother moved in the opposite direction, to Long Island, New York. My father was very frugal and always looked to get the most from his money. He bought a three-family house on Long Island. This is where my brother and I grew up. From Berlin and Munich, Germany, to Newark, New Jersey; then to Long Island, New York. It was quite the culture shock for them.

We still saw Martin, Nadia, and Steven often. They would come out to Long Island and stay over for the weekend and we went to visit them in New Jersey throughout my childhood.

Our new home was a white, Spanish-style stucco house, very different from all the others on the block; but hey, we were extremely different than any other family on the block as well. Our town was predominantly Catholic, with a small Jewish population. Like most people, I do not have too many memories from the first few years of my life. Sometimes I think I buried many of my experiences because of the trauma I went through. I was probably aware in some way about my parents' scheme to get rid of me. My first memory was when I was about two years old. My parents were traveling somewhere in the world and they left me to stay at some distant relatives on my father's side who lived in New York City. I had never met them, and I was leaving my parents' side for the first time. I remember screaming my lungs out. I didn't want to stay there. I didn't know these strangers and I was frightened.

As I got a little older, around three years old, I was a tomboy who loved to climb trees; I was always very physical. Nadia would call me the little monkey. I loved to swim, too, so I was also referred to as a fish. In the summer months you would always find me down the block at the beach, in the water. I was an impish little girl. No one messed with me. I had really short hair, thanks to the so-called hairdresser next door who would always give me a butch cut. She would get one side uneven so she would have to cut the other side to match, and before long it was all cut off. People would mistake me for a boy many times; I had that androgynous look.

I remember teaching myself how to ride a two-wheeler, using a little bike. My parents didn't get involved in our learning to do these things. Back then we played on the streets in and around the block. We didn't know about predators and child molesters then. Life was like *The Adventures of Ozzie and Harriet* or *Leave It to Beaver*. Well, maybe not, but we lived in the illusion of wanting to be like them—perfect families living cookie-cutter lives. But behind closed doors, there were different stories being told, stories that were not so ideal; especially in my home.

We were far from normal; more like *The Outer Limits*. Do not attempt to adjust the dial on your TV. No, it wasn't that bad; it was just different. My father got a job with the airline, TWA, as a steward. His run was from New York to Germany, Paris, or London. In the early 1960s people did not fly in planes as much as they do now. These were the years of early pioneering for commercial air flights. My mom worked as a dressmaker for wealthy women and men. Some of her customers were in the Mafia. I guess you can say she had her own business; however, she always gave her services away too cheaply. It was a shame because she was so talented.

My father was home one week and then gone the next. Most families in the neighborhood had a father with a nine-to-five job and a stay-at-home mom. Neither of my parents were conventional. They had foreign accents, were un-American in nature, and had different customs. Maybe I would have been better off growing up in the city or somewhere else had I been adopted. I liked it when my dad was away. His presence always intimidated me. Hmm, I wonder why? Do you think it had anything to do with him wanting me gone? He was a cold man—or at least that was my impression of him. I never felt any love from either of my parents. They never hugged me or showed any kind of demonstrative affection. I was not told that I was loved and neither was my brother. Looking back, I know they loved us very much; they just didn't know how to show it. They were not taught how to love in a healthy and open way. What our parents don't fix, their children inherit. How could they know how to show love, anyway? Their early years were ripped apart because of the war. They did the best they could with the tools they had; and if they knew better, they would have done better.

Being a little girl I wasn't this philosophical. I did not have a good relationship with my father. Actually I never called him Dad or anything. I just never addressed him, which is really weird to think about. I referred to him as Dada (German for Dad) when I would talk to my mom and brother about him, but I wouldn't say that to him. I had that much fear of him. I always had a really uncomfortable feeling around him. I called my mom Mummy (German for Mommy.)

Growing up, school was always a challenge for me. My brother excelled in school and always made the honor roll and got straight A's. I was the rebellious one, always bucking authority and wanting to do things my way. Little by little, the wild child was chipped out of me. I would love to have part of her back. I loved that free spirited, unafraid child who attempted to dance to the beat of her own drum. I wish I had been encouraged to follow my passion, or had been told how wonderful I was. Every child needs to hear this. Every child needs to know that they are "God seed," that they have the ability to do, be, or have anything they desire if they reach to their fullest potential.

We are miracles in motion. With all my striving and success in my later years, I still have this little insecure girl inside of me, believing that she is not worthy of a great career or fulfillment. Maybe that is why I am waitressing, rather than contributing to something bigger and grander. It is just a reflection, but a rather good insight, I think. I believe that it is important to examine the past, to see where you came from, but not stay there and linger. It is more important to be in the now and set goals and intentions for the future in order to create the life you want to live. I have accepted my past by creating a new future.

I used to play the victim; and boy, did I play her well. I blamed my past for the reason I was so dysfunctional. Now I love my story; I love my past. I look at the happy moments more than the sad ones. I see the sad times as learning experiences and can actually smile while I think of little Karen going through all her struggles. I have compassion for her and I can embrace and love that little girl. I have done a lot of inner child work to heal these wounds that lie deep. Yet the issues are still in my tissues. Like an onion, I am still peeling the layers back, revealing my authentic self.

During my youth, my parents took many vacations. They were able to travel for practically nothing, as my father received many perks while working for TWA. Back in the 1960s, they would put the flight attendants up at the Hilton and give them royal treatments. My mom and dad traveled to parts of the world where most people would never dare to go, like Africa, China, and exotic islands. I went on some of those trips with them; however, they thought I was too difficult for some, so they left me behind with various neighbors from time to time. Despite this, I was able to see places such as Greece, Turkey, Spain, Italy, Germany, England, and Israel, and throughout the United States as well. Sometimes I was left at my grandmother's house in Germany. I always loved that; I felt at home there and it is where some of my fondest memories took place. Other times, when I was left with different families, it was not so pleasant. On the third floor of our house lived the Kempets, Louise and Alfred, and their three children. The apartment was a two-bedroom, one-bath unit. Alfred was from Texas and Louise from Mexico. She made the best tacos in the world! She had her own tortilla press from Mexico and we used to help her make them. Alfred worked for Pan Am as a mechanic and Louise stayed home to raise the children. They were really fun and easy going. I was left to stay with them. The more the merrier; what's one more kid sharing one bathroom and bedroom?

But I often felt very lonely there. I wanted my own family. I saw the Kempets interact with love and security, and this was something my parents were incapable of. Sometimes I was left there on holidays, which made it even worse, knowing my parents were away somewhere. My brother got to travel with them much more often, since he was the quiet one.

I was left with various family friends when my parents travelled. I saw many dynamics of how different families lived. This only made me realize how dysfunctional my own family was.

Whenever I would play with the kids on the block, I was never afraid to get down and dirty. I remember one time I had a fight with Johnny, a neighborhood punk. He was pretty tough, but I was tougher. He didn't expect that I would get the better of him and kick his butt, but I did. We were like two animals on the ground, punching, kicking, pulling hair, and entangled in a ball of fury. I managed to lay into him really good and for a moment was able to free myself long enough to run back home and lock the door. He ran up the steps to where I was, only to see me sticking my tongue out at him from the window. He was so mad I thought he would break the window. I continued to tease him from my safety zone until he disappeared, defeated and humbled, beaten by a girl.

The next day all was forgotten. We didn't seem to hold on to our anger for too long. We were kids, and the fight had probably started for some silly reason, got heated, and then dissipated into the ether from where it began. We played basketball the next day, not even remembering that we'd whopped each other to oblivion. Wouldn't that be great if we could fight like that as adults, and then laugh and play the next day without all the mental torture we put ourselves through by holding on to our pride?

I love the story about the two Indian monks on a pilgrimage who came across a woman struggling to cross a stream without getting her sari wet. One of the monks proceeded to help her by carrying her across the water. As he put her down on the other side of the stream, the woman thanked him, and they all went back on their own paths. A few hours later, the other monk said to the monk who'd carried the woman across, "You know, we are not allowed to touch women and you carried that woman." He replied, "Are you still carrying that woman? I put her down hours ago." We should all practice short-term memory loss; there would be a lot less hostility in our world.

I have learned to do this at the luncheonette. Sometimes I get so angry when a customer is being irritating; but I shake the energy off. I still have to pull out the thorns though. They can go deep and get infected if I don't allow that energy to release itself. It can hurt to pull those thorns out; but if you don't, you will always have a chronic pain gnawing away underneath the surface of your skin, becoming lodged in some vulnerable part of your body and slowly eating away at your energy and power. Ah, the great lessons of life.

———— ⁓⁓ꙮ⁓ ————

Anyway, back to my childhood. Yes, we were young kids playing and having fun. Life was pretty good when my mom was around and my father was off traveling. My brother had many friends and belonged to the Boy Scouts and other organizations. He had a paper route, which I got to take over when he was away traveling with my parents. I, however, was not encouraged to join the Girl Scouts or other clubs. It was like I was brushed to the side somehow, almost invisible at times.

I made my own way, observed how people lived, and used what I could to get by. When my dad was around, life was like walking on egg shells. You never wanted to get him mad. But this demeanor eventually took a toll on him; the wear and tear of everyday life was beginning to eat away at him. Those carefree days of life without children and responsibility were over. Work and all those things that can impact people in a negative way, if they choose to focus on the side of fear, was beginning to impact him. He had many thorns embedded in his mind-body and thus was creating a pain-body. In Eckhart Tolle's book *The New Earth*, he describes how people become addicted to their traumas and their pain. My father was doing just that.

One day, when we were still very young children, my brother was in the dining room where the radio was broadcasting the stock exchange, which my father was very much into. He invested heavily in the markets. I was in the living room playing. My father was listening to the exchange on the radio while lying down in his bedroom, just a small hallway away. Michael began playing with the dials on the radio, like small children love to do. My father went into a rage, came out, and beat the living daylights out of him. This defenseless seven-year-old boy was hit mercilessly. I remember feeling so hurt for my big brother. I went over and held him in my arms. This little four-year-old girl felt the compassion for his heart and soul that was deeply wounded. I cuddled him for a long time until he stopped crying.

My mom was not around that day. If she were, she would not have nurtured him the way I did. She just didn't know how. Somehow, even at four, I knew how; it came so naturally to me. I believe an angel channeled through me to heal my brother. I didn't even have a conscious mind yet; but my subconscious was downloading everything and storing it in the recesses of my mind. That angel has stayed with me to this day.

These are the rages my father had from time to time; but that was the only time he beat my brother. I am sure he felt awful about it afterward, but never said anything about it to anyone. I, on the other hand, felt his backhand often. He had this tiger's eye ring that stung like crazy when he slapped me on my face, which was often. I was the whiner, the needy one, always nagging for something. Of course I was; I wasn't getting the attention I so desperately needed, so I became the squeaky wheel. It was not a good strategy for getting my father's attention. It only made him mad.

Once when I was about eleven, my dad was playing cards with some of his buddies in the same dining room where my brother had gotten that whipping. I asked him if I could sleep over at a girlfriend's house. He was deeply engaged in his cards and was not paying attention to me. There was heavy cigarette smoke in the air, and beer and scotch were the drinks of choice. I kept on nagging him for an answer, which never came. He finally got so boiled up with me pestering him that he picked me up by my hair, kicked me a few times, and then threw me down the stairs, where I had a bedroom at the time. I was furious! I cried my eyes out, screaming out that I hated him. I just kept saying that over and over; I did hate him at the time.

He went back up to play his cards in peace. Peace? I don't think so. That anger, that fierce acid that was burning inside his gut, was manifesting into cancer. He had so much putrefied hostility running through his veins that it had nowhere to go but to become trapped inside of his body. He was addicted to suffering. My father was producing the chemicals, the neuropeptides that would latch on to the receptor sites of his cells, that created an environment conducive to illness.

After that episode, my mom came down to try to console me, but I was not having it. I was becoming an addict myself. I was getting addicted to pain, abuse, and insecurity. The spunky little girl I once was began to hide and this new, confused young girl was emerging. Incident after incident would form the backbone of who I was becoming.

Another poignant memory I have was of a time when Michael and I were staying with our grandparents, Amo and Apo (German for grandma and grandpa), in Munich. We were flying alone back to New York and the plan was to meet my parents at the airport and drive home together. My parents were supposed to arrive at the same time from their own trip. Unfortunately the timing didn't work out exactly as they had planned and Michael and I arrived at Kennedy airport, waiting and looking for our parents, who never showed.

I was only six and Michael nine; he was always so cool and had his wits about him. I was a mess, crying and scared to death in this lonely, cold, and impersonal place with people coming and going without anyone noticing anybody else. Michael took charge and knew that their flight must have been delayed or canceled, so he led the way home like a true Boy Scout who was lost in the woods would. He never spoke a word to reassure me that all would be OK; he just forged ahead and made sure that I was safe. We took a bus back to Long Island, walked down the block and up to the second floor of our home. He must have had a key, or knew where one was, because we got in. And there we waited until they arrived home. I have total amnesia as to when they finally did make it back home. I cried myself to sleep that night, as I often did, and stayed asleep to this memory for a long time.

———— ᘐᖶᴖᕮᵵᴗᕮᵵᴗᴖᗷᘎ ————

My brother and I stayed with my grandparents in Munich often. I have fond memoirs of those times. My maternal grandmother married a very gentle and kind man before I was born, whom I knew as my grandfather. He was a good man and a great grandfather. I really loved him. Too bad I didn't see him often enough. He would take the time to play games with me, take walks, and pay attention to my needs. Sometimes, he would cook for us and we would feast together.

My grandmother was Catholic, and she took me once to visit a church in the center of Munich. It was called The Three Sisters Church. Germany has many beautiful churches with Italian architecture. We went inside this massive house of worship and I was overwhelmed by the size of it. It had a long center aisle leading up to the altar. On both sides of the aisle were large columns extending all the way up to the cathedral ceiling. There were long pews, to sit while a service was being given, with beautiful stained glass windows. Smack in the center of the entrance, right when you walked in, was this embedded mark on the ground. My grandmother told me that it was the devil's footprint. I got so freaked out; after all, I couldn't have been older than seven. She said that the minute the devil saw the light, he vanished. His footprint was precisely at a spot where the columns blocked the windows. If you moved slightly to the left or the right, you saw light. Talk about instilling fear in a child. Oh, my God, I was petrified! I believed the devil to be real. To this day, I'm not sure what that was. It is very spooky.

My grandmother was a real independent thinker. She often told me stories of times during the war when people greeted her in the hall of her apartment house, raised their right hand, and said "Heil Hitler" (That was the standard greeting among the people of that time). She said she'd spit on the ground instead. She would never conform to the Hitler regime. Bless her heart!

———— ∿∾◦◦◦∾∿ ————

My uncle Osker, my grandma's brother, bought a farmhouse in the Black Forest that needed work, and we would go there for a few days when we visited. I loved it there. The house was being renovated and I got to see the improvements every time we went back, which was sometimes more than twice a year.

The first time we saw the place it was pretty basic. No indoor bathroom. There was an old wooden outhouse that really creeped me out. Spiders and funky things were in there; however, I did use it if I had to go. The kitchen had a wood-burning stove that would cook all of our food and we got water from a well nearby.

Carl, the hired hand who lived on the farm, was the most jovial, pleasant, gnome-like man I'd ever met. He must have been missing most of his teeth and he never brushed what was left of his straggly hair. Michael and I would tease him and say we were looking for fleas in his head. He didn't mind.

On the farm, there was a huge pig that gave birth to lots of piglets, a few goats, lambs, ponies, and chickens. We got to feed the baby lambs with bottles. There also was a bird coop with various types of fowl. There was a garden with fruit trees and other edibles on the land.

When we wanted fresh milk, we would have to walk to the next farm, about a mile away. Life on the farm was simple. We had everything we needed; fresh eggs, milk, breads, jams—all good things. The smell of manure is still fresh in my memory. Yes, I felt love there. I felt secure. I felt at home.

Between the nurturing I received from my grandmother and great-uncle, and the peaceful surroundings, I was able to connect to a deep inner peace, one that I can still reconnect with now when I close my eyes and meditate.

Little by little the farmhouse became more modernized. Eventually a bathroom went in along with plumbing, toilets, bathtubs, and sinks. This was a good thing, and I definitely didn't miss that creepy outhouse. They got a television, and I remember everyone sitting around in the family room watching *Bonanza* in German. It seemed so odd to see these cowboys speaking German. There was always gaiety, laughter, playfulness, and light conversation. I wear a ring on my pinky finger that I got from my grandmother one Easter at that farm. I never take this ring off; the energy of the ring is full of love.

It was hard to go back to Long Island after being in this blissful state. At home, life was more serious, and when my father was around, I was on guard. When we would eat dinner my brother and I were not allowed to talk. We had to sit up straight, no elbows on the table, and eat what was on the plate. Sometimes I really didn't like what he made. He liked to cook calf or beef liver, chicken hearts, or cow's tongue. Organ meets were not my idea of tasty food. Yuck!

My dad cooked when he was home, and my mom cooked basic food when he wasn't. My mom was very much like another child that my dad was looking after. To this day, she still is very childlike. My father did the shopping, cleaning, cooking, and all the household maintenance. He paid the bills and did practically everything.

My mom had her small alteration business, so that kept her busy. She was always sewing something and cursing at the same time. She would get frustrated if her sewing machine wasn't cooperating with her. A crazy phrase I would often hear her say was "Zackradeen nomenie." I don't think it really had a meaning, but it let off steam for her while she worked. My father had one, too. If we asked him what was for dinner, he would say "Ingemackluckadodas." I don't think that had a meaning, either. To him it meant whatever is served, and don't ask—just eat it. These two crazy German parents.

My mom had her own temper, too. I saw the brunt of it a few times. Once when I was sitting at the kitchen table with her, she was fixing a hem on a pair of slacks for someone and I was asking her something. She was getting annoyed with my inquisitive nature. To get me to stop, she wanted to hit my hand with her scissors. Well, being the swift kid that I was, I moved my hand to the top of my head. So she then proceeded to aim for my hand, on my head. I saw her coming and quickly moved my hand off my head. She did not react that fast and wham, the scissors landed in my head. Ouch! Blood was gushing all over the place. Boy, did she feel awful. I was in shock! Off to the emergency room we went, where I needed a few stitches.

Another time, when I was about eleven, I was standing in the open doorway between the kitchen and the dining room, and my mom again was sitting at the kitchen table sewing. She was probably frustrated about something, which was causing her to be short-tempered. I was asking her something over and over again, like most children do, and she wasn't giving me the answer I was looking for. I had a way of being very persistent. She threw the scissors at me and they landed in my right thigh. The scissors were sticking out of my leg. I had to pull them out and I had a nice deep wound in my leg. I still have that scar on my thigh. Mommy dearest. Again, she was so sorry and apologetic.

The damage parents can do to their children when they react rather than respond. It took many years for my mom to calm down to the point where she could control her reactions to throw things. It was like a child raising children.

I didn't have it as bad as some children, though. I heard a story at work where a father would take his kids and punish them by sticking their heads in a dirty toilet bowl filled with feces. That is horrible. I can't imagine you can be normal after experiences like that. There is so much abuse, mentally and physically, that parents unthinkingly inflict on their children. I see the way some parents talk to their children at the luncheonette. If we learn how to stop and think, to become conscious of our actions rather than react, we can stop the behavior we were taught and respond in a healthier way. Then the next generation will not have to endure the pain of shame.

---

Because all of the families on my block were Catholic, every Sunday, I would see all of the girls put on their nicest dresses and put kerchiefs on their head. You couldn't go in the church without one at the time. I wanted to fit in so badly that I would do the same, even though I wasn't raised Catholic, Jewish, or anything else. I would walk with them and go to church like all the good girls did. I didn't feel like a good girl inside; I felt different—tainted in some way. I'm not sure what or where that feeling came from, but I just always felt like I wasn't good enough. It probably came from the cellular memory of not being wanted.

I know I didn't want to be associated with being Jewish. There was still quite a bit of anti-Semitism in people's minds and I would be made fun of because some kids knew I was of Jewish background. Regardless of our lack of faith, we celebrated Christmas and always had a Christmas tree when my parents were home and not traveling for the holiday.

When I did get to go along on a trip with my parents, I never wanted to go. I wanted to be normal like all the other kids and stay home with them. I couldn't understand why we had to venture outside the comfort zone of our small town and fly to some foreign place. Now, I look back and think how fortunate I was to have had that privilege to see so many different cultures and lands.

My mom was afraid to fly but somehow got through it. My dad would always go to places where the tourists never went. He loved to travel and see the world for what it was. He was highly self-educated, and spoke French, German, English, and some Italian. My brother has this gift of language as well. Along with English, he speaks French, Italian, Spanish, Germany, Thai, Russian, and some Mandarin. I only speak German and English.

Because the airline business was so new in the early 1960s, we got to experience first-class travel in economy. We had gourmet meals and silverware, a menu that could have come from the finest of restaurants, hot towels, slippers, chewing gum, Colorforms kits to play with, and many other goodies. At that time, people were allowed to smoke on planes, and I often became sick from the smell and poor air quality. I couldn't wait to get off the plane and settle in our hotel room.

We traveled to many places. My paternal grandmother continued to live in England after the war, and I stayed with her a few times while my parents and brother were off on other adventures. She lived with a roommate in Golden's Green, London. It was a Jewish section that was close to the center of London.

I did not get along with this grandmother as well as I did with my maternal grandmother. But I loved, loved, loved, London during the sixties. It was hip, fun, wild, and exciting. This was the time when the Beatles were just coming into their own. Bell bottoms, platform heels, tie-dye clothing, and Afros were all the rage. The energy in the air was buzzing with excitement. Everywhere you went you could feel good vibrations. I loved the fashion, music, dancing, and all the funky stuff that came out of this era. I still consider myself a hippie at heart.

In London, there was this cool department store called Biba. Everybody who was anybody went there. It was like Macy's on steroids. They had so many cool things and it was eye candy to see it all. I was dazzled and intoxicated by it. My grandma, Betty (I didn't call her anything else), was so proper and old fashioned and didn't like the clothing that I was wearing with all the style that was coming out. I was about twelve or thirteen by this time. She also did not like me sleeping past a certain time in the morning. We would have these fights where she would pull the covers off me and I would pull them back over me. This would go on for a few minutes until I gave in and got up, disgruntled. She always got her way.

I can see why my father had a hard time mending their relationship, which had been torn apart when they went their separate ways during the war. They were never close; though they somehow managed to heal their wounds, at least superficially.

I had in one sense this beautiful life: traveling and seeing the world with educated parents who believed in striving to discover the diversity of the world. I grew up without prejudice, and was taught manners and respect for our earth. I saw the finer things in life, often stayed in four-star hotels, and ate some of the best cuisine from around the world. I was exposed to people who were scholars and listened to stimulating conversations.

On the flip side, I had this dysfunctional life in a small town that was not very progressive. Where did I fit in? My parents did the best job that they knew how in raising my brother and me, I truly know this now. Like me, they were torn between two worlds. They didn't know how to reach out and ask for help. They couldn't go on the internet and do a Google search for information about personal development. They just didn't have the resources that we do today.

This was a time of massive change. Everything was between worlds. In the old world, the atom had been dropped on Hiroshima and Nagasaki and tens of thousands of people had been killed. But the war never ended; it had just changed locations in the new world.

The nuclear family was being birthed. Einstein's formula, his life-changing equation $E=mc^2$, was still being adopted. Quantum physics was baffling the most brilliant scientists. Questions like "How can an electron act as a particle and a wave at the same time?" were being pondered. String theory, wormholes, psychedelic drugs, revolution in the streets, and the equal rights movement were all rising. We were discovering our true nature and yet simultaneously moving further away from it.

There was unrest in the air, and the music was reflecting it. The deep, soulful lyrics of the times were creating provocative questions as to why and what we are doing to each other and to the world.

Back home, in my little world, I was oblivious to all of this. I remember seeing *The Wizard of Oz* on television for the first time; I was totally mesmerized. When Dorothy landed in Oz and everything turned from black and white to color, it was awesome. This is still one of my favorite movies, and I love to watch it every year around the holidays. It is so full of symbolism and deep meaning. We all have a scarecrow, tin man, and lion in our lives. We all have angels or spirits who assist us if we call on them. We can all find our way home when we are lost, if we search within ourselves. We just have to remember who we really are and awaken to this wisdom and knowledge. Just click your heels three times and repeat, "There's no place like home."

Home is where the heart is; but my home never felt like home. I never got that warm, cozy feeling from being there. I moved around from one family's home to another. Home was inside me.

# CHAPTER 5

As a child, I had an imaginary friend that I would have long conversations with in the bathroom. I would lock myself in there if I got mad at my mother, and then I'd clean the bathroom. I had a thing for cleaning. It was really weird, but it helped me calm down, and my mom didn't mind, either. Then when it was nice and clean, I would sit down on the closed toilet seat and have very serious conversations with my friend. We would talk about all sorts of things and I felt safe and at home there with her. She understood me. She didn't have a name. Whenever I needed to console myself I knew I could always go into the bathroom and find her. I believe she was one of my angels. Thank God for her presence in my life, since I didn't have my parents' support or guidance to show me the way. She was there for me when I needed her.

We had a neighbor across the street, an elderly man by the name of David. He had beautiful roses that he looked after in his front garden. I love the smell of tea roses. But David was a dirty old man. It is so ironic that he cared for these beautiful flowers, because he was so filthy himself. He would entice my girlfriends and me over to his house and offer us candy for a kiss, a cheap feel down our pants and up our shirts. My friends, Marilyn, Aileen, and I would go over there, tempted by the candy. I had a voracious sweet tooth and prostituted myself for the goodies, as did the other girls. I didn't care that much, as long as I got what I wanted: the candy!

I would never tell my parents about this. I just couldn't talk about this to them. We were only about seven years old at the time. We didn't have any sexual feelings and he didn't make us touch his penis or any other body parts, so it didn't seem so bad. Marilyn eventually did tell her mother, and she put a stop to David's shenanigans. I was glad that she spoke up, because although I loved the candy, he really gave me the creeps. He only got a slap on the hand and a scolding from Marilyn's mother. Today it would have been a much bigger deal. He would have been prosecuted as a child molester.

My prostitute archetype revealed herself very early in my life. According to Jungian psychology, we all have these archetypes within us. Caroline Myss, a world-renowned and respected lecturer in the field of health, intuition, and contemporary spirituality, points out that all humans have four archetypes in common—the prostitute, the victim, the child, and the saboteur. There are other archetypes as well, but I know and am aware when any of these four are lurking behind the scenes, trying to pull me into the drama of their characters. I acknowledge their presence when they reveal themselves to me. I can even thank them now, for letting me know what I need to be conscious of in the moment and what I might be playing out, if I allow them to run loose in a particular situation. It takes practice to observe oneself and understand what the consequences of one's actions might be. There are lessons to be learned, and life presents them to us when we need them most. Earth school 101.

The appearance of the prostitute archetype does not necessarily mean we are giving our bodies away, for money or other things we want. It could mean we are in a dead-end relationship or a job we do not like in exchange for comfort, safety, or a salary. The point is to become aware of our actions and then decide if this is something we want to continue. Perhaps they are serving us for the time being. The fact that we get to choose is our greatest gift. At any time we can choose and then decide to change or not. The choices we make will ultimately dictate how our lives will turn out. This was a huge lesson for me and one that I am still practicing. I have made some choices that were not of my highest good at times. I have since learned to follow my intuition.

———————

One time Marilyn, Aileen, and I walked into town to shop for something, probably candy. It was just about dusk and we were heading home when a man in a parked car called us toward him. My radar went wild with vibes saying, "Stay away." Aileen and Marilyn were much more trusting and were ready to approach him, when I said, "No way; let's just run home and make lots of noise while we do it."

Sure enough the guy got spooked and drove off in a hurry. Following my intuition probably saved our lives. I didn't always listen and follow it as I grew older. However, I have now learned to honor my strong gut feelings and listen much more carefully. It is usually a very subtle feeling or vibe that you will sense somewhere in your body. For me I sense it in my stomach, which is where our second brain is.

Intuition is a mental muscle that, like any other muscle, can be strengthened with practice. You can begin by playing a game with yourself. Whenever your phone rings, ask yourself "I wonder who that is?" and take a guess. You can get very good at this. You can think of someone and all of a sudden they will call or show up. Practice; its fun, and so vital to living in today's complicated world. Your intuition is like a good friend that will assist you in navigating the rough seas when the storms of your life swell up. It is your internal compass.

———— ⚬⚬⚬⚬⚬⚬⚬ ————

Down the street from me lived the Mulligans, They were older and were like my surrogate grandparents. I adored them. I don't think they had any children of their own so they invited me over to their home from time to time when I was very young. I would sometimes eat lunch there and play in their garden. They had a nice, well-maintained yard and they were such a calming influence in my life.

I felt so comfortable there. It was as if I learned how to meditate in their home. Time stood still around them, even though I was too young to have a sense of time. I felt ageless, free, loved, cared for, and secure. I could just sit for hours in one of their rocking chairs and be happy. It was the aura of their home; it was full of peace. I always did my best to recreate this feeling in any of my homes when I became an adult. But it was them. I felt they had some essence that permeated the walls, the furniture, and everything else around them. I was different around them. The rambunctious and sassy little girl that I was changed into someone else. I loved the stillness that came over me.

I didn't realize it at the time, but all those personalities were in me all along. We are all full of these different personae, these archetypes that make up who we are. We just need to know how to harness them and integrate them all into one whole being, without having them be scattered about. Sometimes I can be the mischievous child or the sweet, calm young lady; at other times I can become the healer or the pioneer woman. They are all a part of who I am.

The pioneer archetype came out of me when my family would take trips to upstate New York. Martin and Nadia had bought an old farmhouse there—sixty acres of land, with a fresh stream running through it. They would go up almost every weekend to renovate it. It was a small, Cape Cod-like house, with two bedrooms upstairs and an open living space on the first floor. A wood-burning stove kept us warm during the cold nights.

They dredged out some land and created a pond just meters from the house that was fed by the natural stream on the property. They also built a one-room guest house right by the pond. Freshwater fish were stocked so they could go fishing at any time. Frogs soon found their way to these waters, which I loved. I was fascinated by the frogs and would watch them for hours, as their babies morphed from tadpoles to frogs.

I would sometimes take a frog out of the water and dissect it. I just wanted to see what was inside of them. I know it seems cruel, but I was so curious about these reptilian creatures. I would carefully remove their little hearts while they still had a beat, and saw the increased pulsation when I sprinkled salt on them. It was so interesting. I don't know why I had this fascination with frogs, but I still do have an affinity for them. I feel sorry that I hurt them; however, a young curious mind will explore and experiment at will. Besides, that was all the entertainment I had. My parents were always doing something together with Martin and Nadia, Steven was off with my brother, and I was left to my own devices. The frogs became my friends, and sometimes my lab guinea pigs. I didn't always do this; most of the time I just observed them in the water, trying to catch one, and then setting it free. The metamorphosis that occurred from being fish-like to being a frog is what drew me toward studying them.

There was this treehouse that my brother and Steven built on the edge of the stream that I became very attached to. When they weren't using it, I would climb up it and make it my fortress. I imagined all sorts of things up there. I made a pulley system with a rope and tin can that I slowly lowered into the stream, filled with water, and reeled back up. There I made soups and different concoctions of all kinds.

I pretended I was a pioneer woman. I forged for berries and lived off the land. I was strong, independent, and used my ingenuity. It was a magical place for me to surrender to my wild side. I also got to practice my imagination, another mental muscle that is vital to manifesting what you desire in life. Einstein said "imagination is more powerful than knowledge," and I happen to agree with him. I was learning survival skills on my own, too, and I was a naturalist. I was never squeamish about things. I didn't mind getting dirty and being barefoot; I actually preferred it. Spiders creeped me out (and still do); however, I had a high respect for them, as long as they kept their distance.

I had to adapt to spending much of my time alone whenever we went to visit the Lebersteins. Whether it was visiting them at their farmhouse upstate or their home in New Jersey, I was always the odd man out. Michael had Steven, my father had Martin, and my mom had Nadia. I had me, myself, and I. The farmhouse was full of nature so I was always involved in some kind of quest. Besides frogs, ants were another fascination of mine. When they gathered together by the thousands, one on top of the other in this big frenzy of activity, it would spur my interest. It seemed like one big, black, moving ball on the ground. On closer inspection, I would notice there was some sort of food supply that they were all breaking apart, and they were taking turns, bringing it back to their underground home.

Of course I couldn't let things be as they may; I had to disrupt their hard work by blowing on them to see what would happen. They probably thought a twister was blowing through and they picked up speed. The harder I blew the faster they moved. It was like I could control them. Aha—I discovered I had this power. I didn't want to hurt them, just play with and control them in some bizarre way. They took care of their injured ones. I observed how some of them would carry a wounded ant back down to their nest. It seemed like they had an orderly system, which I later learned they do.

The natural world is amazing and the more we learn to respect and take care of it, the more we will discover our deep connection to it. So many people have become completely detached from this source of energy. It is vital to our existence here on this beautiful planet Earth.

When we occasionally visited New Jersey, I didn't have the resources I had when I was at the farm. Here, there were kids to play with, but I always felt uncomfortable around them. My insecurities surfaced. I felt different and I had a tough time assimilating. I wanted my fortress back. I wanted to run for shelter in my treehouse. I wanted the frogs, ants, and other natural elements.

I would often just retreat back into their house and watch TV. Being alone was more comfortable to me. Back home, I didn't have this issue because I was in control; it was my neighborhood and I knew the kids, I knew how to maneuver around situations and people. Here, I didn't have this control. I also felt this way in school. On the streets of my neighborhood, I was confident; but in the confines of an institutional setting with authoritarian figures, I would morph into a shy, bashful girl. It was another side to my personality. Like the tadpoles, I too could morph into something else.

The Lebersteins' home looked like a mini palace to me. Their house was new and had all the latest gizmos in it; everything seemed so large and everything was new. Not like my house, where we had a lot of secondhand goods and older appliances. It seemed like they were rich, and I really liked it. I wanted to have these things. Life seemed to be good for them on the surface, but like many families, underneath it all were hidden tales of depression and confusion lurking in the recesses of their minds, waiting for the opportunity to reveal themselves.

# CHAPTER 6

When the Lebersteins' son Steven turned thirteen, he had his bar mitzvah. It was a lavish celebration. I was eleven, and I remember dancing up a storm to the live band that was performing. I took advantage of any opportunity I got to dance. I loved to move and I was always the first one on the dance floor. I never cared if anyone was watching or not. It was in my bones to dance and I was always the hit of the party. All the girls came up to me in the bathroom and wanted to know if I took dancing lessons and how I was able to dance so well.

I couldn't believe the reception I was getting. This was the first time I was so popular. It felt good to know that I was gifted in something. From that point on, I became aware of my unique ability and was very conscious every time I got to dance in public. Every time I did, I was applauded for my dancing skills, which were all self-taught. It is a natural gift that God has given me and I am so grateful for it. We all have our unique gifts; they just need an outlet to be expressed and shared with the world.

---

Unlike my friends, I never had any rite of passage, like a bat mitzvah or a confirmation. I believe that rites of passage are important to celebrate milestones, achievements, unions, or any other significant changes that may be taking place in our lives. They are symbolic to understanding who we are, where we came from, and where we are heading. They are metaphorically allowing our transition to taking on a more responsible role in life.

I did travel to Israel with my father when I was thirteen. This was one of the best memories I have of being with him. He was actually a great guy during this trip, and it was only the two of us. Go figure! This is exactly what I had craved and longed for. He had relatives living in Jerusalem at the time, so we were able to stay with them. I swam in the Dead Sea and I literally had to shake the salt from my body when I got out. It was amazing, the level of saline in the water; you couldn't sink if you wanted to. Although it has amazing healing properties, nothing can live in these waters; that is why they call it the Dead Sea. I have since visited many areas where there are natural healing waters, like the Blue Lagoon in Iceland and sulfur spas in New Zealand. I believe my visit to the Dead Sea was the beginning of my attraction to natural healing waters.

In Jerusalem I got to visit the Golden Mosque. It is a very holy place and according to Judaic tradition, it is the symbolic foundation upon which the world was built and the place of the binding of Isaac. There were markets in the streets and many strange and foreign people. We visited the Wailing Wall and witnessed the suffering of people coming here to pray. The cries that were released from their souls echoed through the air and etched themselves into the depth of my being.

I considered this trip to Isreal my rite of passage. I was able to understand my heritage and appreciate the history of my Jewish ancestry. After all, my last name would have been Israel if my father hadn't changed it. Although I am not religious, I respect others' rights to worship whatever denomination that calls to them. I am a spiritual being. I believe in an infinite intelligence, which I choose to call God. I believe in "Christ consciousness" and the teachings of Jesus, Buddha, Mohammed, and other luminaries who lived for unity and peace. Christ consciousness is the growing human recognition and blending of the human mind with the divine. I believe as our awareness grows we become more liberated, joyful, peaceful, and loving. I have studied theology, a Course in Miracles, the Kabbalah, and other philosophies of living a spiritual life.

I am fascinated by different cultures and mythology. They are all different; yet the same. Different stories, lands, cultures, languages, foods, and currency, from the past to the present, represent the vast diversity that this planet inhabits. Just like all the fauna and flora of our world, it is rich with intricate variations. Life is beaming everywhere. It wants to thrive. So why does it seem like man tries to destroy it? Why do we harm each other?

We are at a crossroads in our world today. Our planet is ailing. Our environment, our water, our soil has been stripped of nutrients and replaced by chemicals. We have genetically modified organisms (GMOs), high fructose corn syrup, hormones, and other artificial ingredients in our foods. Fish are being raised in farms since we have over-harvested the seas. The honey bees are dying, due to monoculture. Insecticides are being sprayed on our fruits and vegetables, and the planet is heating up due to global warming. We have the technologies to seed the skies and produce rain or drought, Monsanto has a monopoly on the crops we grow, and our oceans are full of plastic and garbage. Our carbon footprint is the size of Big Foot, or maybe that devil in the Three Sisters Church. When will we end the madness?

It is astonishing that I can have a conversation with someone in the luncheonette about climate change and they still believe that it is just some hoax. They think the weather is cyclical, and therefore this is normal. They think that these huge storms—like hurricane Sandy, which ripped through and devastated Long Island and other coastal areas in October 2012—are a rare occurrence. What they don't realize is that these weather patterns are becoming more and more common; and they are not representative of a normal, healthy climate. The world is changing; we are evolving. We need to wake up to the reality that life is fragile and precious. Like a caterpillar that must almost die to be reborn as a butterfly, we too are dying.

What will we morph into? I believe we are evolving into crystal-based humans. In other words, we are changing on a cellular level. We are letting go of our three-dimensional world and moving to one of four-dimensions. We are becoming lighter—emotionally, spiritually, and physically. I believe that deep down inside of us, we are encoded to reach higher and become fully multi-sensory. Our DNA is shaped like a spiral and, just like a stairway to heaven, we are revolving internally as well as externally, outward and upward. Everything is connected and there is no separation between us and nature. Like the atom that was split, creating a massive explosion and destruction, the energy is immense when it is whole and contained.

At no other time in human history have we had the greatest potential to change the world and live out our dreams and desires, like we do today. We are the creators; but most of society has not woken up to this truth. Now is the time to emerge from our slumber and become the alchemists that we were born to be, transmuting base metals, or our menial existence, into gold, or our enlightenment.

In Israel at age thirteen, I was so blessed to have had this one time to spend with my father where he was actually was relaxed and loving. Unfortunately, when we arrived back home the pressures of life resurfaced and he resorted back to his old patterns. He didn't blow his cool all the time. It was only when he was under pressure. When someone is under pressure, if they do not have the tools to know how to defuse it, they will blow. Although I walked on eggshells when he was home, I did love him very deeply. I always asked God to keep him safe when he had to travel for work. I would say, "Dear God, please let him have a safe trip going wherever he is going, a safe time where he is staying, and also a safe trip back home." I made sure I included every part of his trip and not leave anything out. These were my prayers for him.

# CHAPTER 7

I was now thirteen, a young lady, although I did not feel like one. I was a late bloomer and my body didn't really mature until about sixteen years of age. Shortly after our trip to Israel, my parents and my brother went off on a trip somewhere and I was left at Hilda Fritz's house. She lived about two blocks from my home, but it felt like I traveled an eternity to hell that time I stayed there. She had an attraction to a boy across the street from her. He was a bad, bad boy. He had evil tendencies. They introduced me to Carbona, a type of cleaning fluid. He had us inhale the fumes on a piece of cloth and we passed out. He then raped us.

That was my first sexual experience. It was not a very pleasant introduction to this sacred act. I was never the same after that.

Hilda and I got high on Carbona a few more times when I would stay at her house. We could have died. I remember passing out completely, being unconscious for minutes; it was crazy. This is what happens to children when they are unsupervised and left to their own devices. Her parents were not around and she was able to get away with all kinds of things without getting caught. I never did this at my house, only there.

I never told my parents about what had happened with that boy. I was too embarrassed and full of shame to talk about it. I am sure my parents would have been devastated and outraged if I had told them. I just didn't have the level of trust or security I needed in order to share this with them, or anyone, for that matter. It was my dirty little secret that I learned to stuff into the recesses of my subconscious mind, hidden away, only to become exposed when I needed to hurt myself again.

That was the pattern that began to develop. I became a shy teenager. At fourteen, I was still small and underdeveloped. However, there were boys who saw the sexy Karen emerging underneath the façade of my appearance. One boy in particular would stop while I was at my locker getting some books and would stroke the back of my hair, telling me how beautiful I was going to be. I didn't know what he saw or if he was just teasing me, but he seemed like he really meant it. He would do this on several occasions and I just allowed him to continue without saying a word.

When Steven was visiting, he and my brother would tease me terribly. Steven was so cruel. He said things like, "I've seen bigger tits on dogs," and he would take my training bras (why I had them, I have no idea) and hang them all over my room. I had to defend myself against their merciless attacks by lying on my bed and kicking really fast and hard. They loved to use me as their punching bag.

In a way, I think it was Steven's way of flirting with me, but I didn't want any part of it. He did this one other time when we were all at the farm upstate. Somehow we were alone in the house and he got me pinned down on the bed in one of the upstairs bedrooms. He was wrestling with me and trying to pull down my pants. I was definitely not going to let this happen and fought back. I was pretty strong for a scrawny young girl. He never did get to do it and eventually gave up. Do boys just have this primal urge to want to dominate any woman they think they can?

I know that hormones play a huge role in teenagers and that sex is definitely a priority on their minds. I was such a late bloomer that these hormones didn't become active until around sixteen years of age. When I did develop, Steven and my brother just shut their mouths. I became this really hot, sexy young lady. In some ways I knew it, from the reactions I received from the boys, but my self-esteem was so low I never fully embraced the magnitude of my gorgeous self.

My self-worth was never healthy. I believe this must have begun from the time I was in my mother's womb and I knew vibrationally that I was unwanted. This pattern would reveal itself over and over again. School would reinforce this behavior. Starting in the first grade, I would always get caught for doing something and be punished for it. My teacher wanted to set an example and embarrass me in front of the class. Really, an example for five- and six-year-olds? I guess she had control issues.

I was in the first grade when President John F. Kennedy was killed. I remember that all of a sudden the news was coming over the loudspeakers and the teacher began to cry. I don't think we understood what was happening but all of us children began to cry, too, and we were sent home from school.

These were the days of practicing duck-and-cover, in case an atom bomb was dropped. Ah, yes, nothing like warping young, fragile, developing minds. Men were landing on the moon, the media was advertising all the latest and greatest gizmos and gadgets, and conformity and consumerism were commonplace. I received many mixed messages in school, at home, and on the news. I was absorbing and downloading all of what I heard, saw, and felt around me.

I never really liked school because I didn't like to conform. It was like I had to be and act like someone I wasn't. My best year was in third grade. Mrs. Weber was an amazing teacher.

She was the one and only teacher who got me. She was always so gentle and nice. That's exactly what I needed. I didn't do well with authoritarian rule. I always responded to a kind and gentle approach. I believe we all do, really. I strived to do better in her class because she always praised me and my work. I was eager to rise above. When you have a mentor or someone who shows you that you are good, it can change the direction of your life. I am grateful for her guidance and her kindness; she was an angel.

Unfortunately, my fourth grade teacher was not on the same wave length as Mrs. Weber, as she had cruel tendencies. I really liked her and always wanted to please her for some reason. She was young, pretty, and had a good sense of style. My mother actually did some alteration work for her and she came over my house to get some clothes measured. While on the surface she seemed nice, underneath it all she had this mean streak.

One day I had forgotten my homework so she proceeded to embarrass me in front of the whole class by telling everyone that I was not smart enough to be in the fourth grade. She had me escorted to a third-grade class, where I had to sit in the back of the room until lunch. I cried my eyes out the whole time; I was so humiliated. My eyes were so red and sore from crying even when I got home on lunch break. My father was home, but either he didn't notice or didn't ask, and I never told him because I was too ashamed and embarrassed. I just stuffed my feelings inwards, as I had learned so well to do. There was so much hurt that my poor little heart had to endure.

The years went by and eventually, I learned how to conform. Well, not totally. That rebellious spirit never did get completely squished, thank God! The following year I had a teacher who again tried to knock my spirit down; however, my feisty nature was able to retaliate. My mom had made me a miniskirt, which I wore to school one day. The teacher said I needed to call my parents to come pick me up and that I needed to change my outfit, as it was inappropriate school attire. Girls were not allowed to wear pants yet, only skirts or dresses. Well, I broke the code, because no one was home to pick me up. I got to stay in class wearing my mini. After that, other girls decided they wanted to wear minis, too. That was the year all of us girls rebelled and began wearing pants. Because we were united in our actions, and we all wore pants together, we were able to create a new rule. It was awesome! Girl power—we rocked!

But this was the year my grandpa Apo died, too. I was called out of class by my brother and he told me the news. It was the first person close to me who died. I remember crying and feeling the pain of his death.

---

The next few years of my life seemed to flow without anything that stood out. I was put in a special class from sixth to eighth grade. A few students would meet for about an hour once a day. It was for kids they labeled as having problems. Gee, I wonder how they came to that conclusion? My brother was three years ahead of me and was just whizzing through school, getting straight A's and always making the honor roll. I wasn't a bad student but was certainly not a straight A student. B's and C's were more my speed. I had problems that prevented me from achieving the success my brother was having. He was a math genius. He played the saxophone really well, too.

I played the violin; however, my mom said it was like nails on a chalkboard or a cat screeching. As you can see, my parents were not so supportive of me. The only praise I ever recieved was when I would dance. When Martin was around and I was dancing to some rock song, he or my dad would say, "She is going to wind up as a dancer in a strip club." I didn't know what that meant at the time, but I learned pretty quickly. I had a way of gyrating my body that was very sensual, even at my young age and with my formless physique. Again, mixed messages, and certainly the wrong ones.

———⟶∿∿◦◖◗◦◖◗◦∿∿———

When I started high school, I joined all the kids' who were shipped off to a school out of town. Our town didn't have a high school, and no other school in the area took us. So we traveled by bus for about half an hour. It seemed like a good school. Of course my brother was excelling. He was in his last year of high school when I was just starting. He had already been accepted to a prestigious school for Engineering.

I had a difficult time adjusting to this big school with so many more students, stimuli, and energy. Again my grades were average; except for math, which I actually did really well in. I got through ninth grade without any real struggle. This would be the last year that anything seemed remotely normal. Little did I know at the time, my world was about to get blown apart like an atom bomb being set off inside of me.

# CHAPTER 8

I remember the fall of 1971 like it was yesterday. I was in the kitchen feeling sorry for my cat, who wasn't feeling well. My father, who was also in the kitchen, said to me, "Don't you care about me?"

I said, "What's wrong with *you*?"

I never thought my father could be sick. After all, fathers are like rocks, even if I didn't get along with him. He said that he didn't feel well. I just blew it off, not thinking any more about it. My brother was already off at college at the time, so it was just my mom, dad, and me at home. The next thing I remember, I was sitting in math class at school and someone came into the class, calling me into the office.

My mom was there to pick me up. She was crying hysterically. She told me that Dada had cancer. I didn't even know what cancer was. When I got home, she said that he had gone to the hospital for tests and they said he had to be operated on immediately. I was confused and in total shock. I just didn't understand, and I had no one to talk to about it.

I did what had always worked best for me; I shoved my feelings deep down into my gut and subconscious mind where no one could find them. I was good at putting up a stoic front. I was able to handle it, I told myself, I was tough!

After they operated on my dad, he was never the same. It was horrible. The image of my father after the surgery was of a weak, sick, depleted man. They removed most of his colon and part of his liver. They gave him a colostomy bag, which totally took away his manhood. At that time, they didn't screen the blood that was donated like they do today for AIDS and other infectious diseases. Since he needed a blood transfusion, he ended up recieving blood that was tainted with something that gave him hepatitis. He became completely jaundiced after being home for a week. His eyes and skin were discolored and he was so fragile and thin that his appearance frightened me.

I was so sad. My mom nearly lost it, but she devoted herself to helping him get better. She had always been a health buff, and she tried to get my father on a holistic regime. She bought a juicer and started making special blends of juices. She went to the library and researched alternative cures. I believe that if my father had been compliant, it would have helped; but he was not ready to change his ways and submit to a new lifestyle. He did quit smoking and drinking the cocktails that he had enjoyed now and again. I don't even remember what he ate, but it couldn't have been much, because he became so emaciated.

Since no one was there to supervise my teenage years, I decided to take the plunge and go all out in self-destructive behaviors. After all, my father said to me many times, "You will be the death of me". Deep down inside of me, I thought maybe I really did cause his illness. I was confused and depressed, and I felt so alone.

Now, I was this sexy, petite, and vulnerable young teen. I didn't know where to turn, so I took the path of least resistance: sex, drugs, and rock 'n' roll. Bring it on! School was the last thing on my mind; though I did manage to get through it. I began to attract the rebellious kids and wanted to associate with them. I started smoking pot and it soon became a daily habit. It was a great escape. I would smoke before school early in the morning and sit in class completely stoned.

The kids that I was hanging out with were all doing it; drinking and getting high was our way of life. Many of us were flunking school. We decided that conventional school was not the route we were interested in taking, so we protested. Since there were quite a large number of us, the administration heard our appeal and we were granted permission to start an alternative school within the same building, using a different curriculum. We named it SAFE. There must have been around thirty to forty of us students. Some of the teachers were brought over to SAFE to be our instructors. We basically had free range, and it was accepted. We had a lounge room where we hung out, smoked cigarettes, and engaged in basically whatever we wanted. There was a lot of drug activity taking place in the bathroom of that lounge.

When I think of the school, it amazes me that we were able to pull this off. We chose the subjects we wanted to learn. We had sewing classes, existential philosophy, and improvisational acting classes. There were no math classes or any other conventional subjects. I am not sure how I even graduated. Most of the time I didn't even go to school. I just got high and hung out at the homes of friends who lived nearby.

Besides pot, I was introduced to Quaaludes, which were various types of muscle relaxants and sedatives. My body and mind took to them like a custom-made glove. I had found the key to releasing all the anxiety within me. I always was so high-strung, and these white pills were able to make me feel relaxed and at ease. However, as with all drugs, the effects were short-lived and when the high was over I needed more of them, more often.

I never became an addict, only an abuser. I would often mix Quaaludes with alcohol, a potentially lethal combination. If I weren't so young and stupid I probably would have been dead by now. Somehow by the grace of God, I lived through these turbulent years. God had bigger plans for me.

There were many parties, late nights, and staying out all night, getting sick from too much booze and drugs. My mom would be worried sick over not knowing where I was. I would forget to call home, and there were certainly no cell phones at the time. I didn't care.

It wasn't long before other drugs were introduced to me: acid and mescaline. Now these were drugs that took my mind for a ride. Where quaaludes relaxed my body and mind, acid and mescaline stimulated me. Wow, a new altered reality. This was awesome. I was tripping my brains out. Talk about lions, tigers, and bears, oh my. I saw things I never saw before. I could go here, there, and everywhere.

By this time, my father was feeling somewhat better and sometimes he was well enough to go back to work. My mom would travel with him and I was left home alone. This was a recipe for disaster. I would have big parties at my house. Even my brother came home from college and partied with me. We had all kinds of wild crazy stuff going on. People were having sex in our bedrooms, smoking and burning holes on the floor, and distributing and ingesting drugs of all sorts. All kinds of wild activities were taking place. We cleaned up as best we could, but my father always knew something had gone on because of the burnt holes on the linoleum floor, along with some broken items and missing things. After all, I was only fifteen, and they'd left me alone. My brother was a bit older but hey, he partied, too. He was able to get away with so much more than I was. I always seemed to take the brunt of the punishment.

It was in the summer of 1973 when I met a young man who took my breath away. I fell in love. It wasn't lust; it was most definitely love, because when I think of him to this day, my heart still skips a beat. Daniel. He was about five years older than me and I was head over heels for him. He really liked me, too. He was a surfer, a pot head, and absolutely gorgeous! I would see him from time to time when I would go visit a friend who lived next door to him. We flirted back and forth until one day he asked me out. Of course I said yes.

I was so excited and couldn't wait to see him and spend a night with him. I remember wanting to look my best and primping myself. I had curlers in my hair and was deciding what to wear when the doorbell rang.

My brother was home from college and working as a waiter at a steak house at a nearby restaurant. My mom was out that day, probably at a customer's house doing some alterations, and my father was not feeling well so he was sleeping in his bedroom. It was late afternoon, around five o'clock, when the doorbell rang. I answered it. There were two grown men standing on my porch. They said they were detectives and proceeded to show me their badges. Yikes! They asked if anyone was home, and I lied and said no. I didn't want to disturb my father because I knew he was not well. One of them said, "Come with me." I wasn't sure what was going on but I followed them outside to our backyard. I had the big curlers still in my hair and I felt like a midget compared to these guys. There were these marijuana plants that my brother had planted back there. One of the detectives pulled them up out of the soil and asked me whose plants they were. I played stupid and said I didn't even know they were there. (I knew they were my brother's). I said that it was a three-family house and people used our back yard as a shortcut. The Post Office and a tenement house were on the other side of our backyard, so anybody could have come and planted them there.

The detectives knew my brother and knew where he was working. They wanted to come into my house and look around. I had the wits about me to ask them if they had a search warrant. (I must have been watching some good detective movies to know to ask this question.) They said that they would come back with one. I was able to dodge a bullet for the time being. I knew my brother was dealing at the time and had pounds of pot and some pills in the house. He was always very industrious and knew how to earn money through various businesses.

I called him at work and told him what had happened. I demanded that he get his ass home ASAP to clean this stuff out. He did. He was home in a flash and got rid of all the stuff in the house. Those bastards did come back, too.

This time my father answered the door. He was so weak and sick. I felt so sorry for him. I sat on my father's recliner in the living room while one of the cops yelled at me, "I thought you said no one was home!"

I was about to say something when my father stood up for me and said, "Leave her alone!"

They wanted to search our house. They were snooping around the living room and noticed all the plants that were scattered about. My mom was way ahead of her time and had lots of indoor plants. They thought this unusual and odd, I guess, but my father somehow convinced them to not search the house. They did, however, take my father down to the precinct. I couldn't believe they did this. He was so sick and they made him go. I was so upset and nervous.

I eventually went out on my first date with Daniel, later that same evening. We just hung out at his house in his room and talked. I told him what happened and we just relaxed into each other's arms and got to know each other on a deeper level. We knew we were going to be with each other for some time. The chemistry was intense. After a few dates together we eventually made love and it was so beautiful. I was so happy in one sense and so depressed in another. I was in love with Daniel. But as I was gaining one man, I was losing another, my father. All I wanted to do was escape all the hurt, sadness, and pain that seemed to penetrate the space within my home. Daniel was a great divergent. I was so comfortable in his presence. This is where I wanted to stay forever, away from the reality of cancer, sickness, and death.

I loved having an exclusive boyfriend. I was not the type of girl who dated many guys. I didn't like having to put on airs or pretend to be interested in anyone when I wasn't. I really enjoyed monogamy. Daniel was extremely handsome and girls flirted around him all the time. This made me anxious. I was very jealous and didn't have much self-confidence, so I felt really confused and hurt when this happened. Daniel also was a flirt and when he engaged in and reciprocated these playful overtures, I was devastated. I did what I did best—retreat into my own world. I would hide myself away and cry, feeling sorry for myself, reinforcing my low self-esteem. I wasn't good enough, pretty enough, or smart enough. This was my modus operandi. This archetype of the hurt child would surface throughout my life.

I was sixteen now. My father was still very sick; however, he managed to work periodically and fly back and forth to Europe. How he did this, I have no idea. This was his joy and what kept him going. He would have died much sooner if he couldn't travel. It gave him his purpose to live. It is amazing what the human spirit can do when it has a strong desire. If only he could have healed his emotional wounds, maybe his physical ones might have recovered as well. He never was able to dig deep into his pain to uncover the cause of his suffering. So he just managed to live out the rest of his young life with the gnawing knowledge of cancer eating away at his body with what I called "dis-ease" in his mind.

My mom was only forty-five, with so much life still in her; but she had nowhere to express her sensuality. I'm sure there was no sex left in their relationship. My father couldn't have sex; he was too weak and sick. My mother began seeing someone. I didn't know who and I didn't want to know. All I knew was that she was out a lot when my father wasn't around.

One summer day my father was just coming home from a trip abroad. He must have caught on that my mom was seeing someone. I remember him waiting in the driveway for her to come home. I could see the looming anger on his face. He asked me if I knew where she was, and I said no, I didn't. I was waiting for Daniel to pick me up, which he did moments later. I was so scared. I knew something bad was going to take place. A few hours later, Daniel was dropping me off in front of my house and all I could hear was my mother screaming in pain. My father was beating her. I asked Daniel to wait in his car while I went into the house for a minute to see what was going on. I went in the house briefly and saw him whipping my mom with a belt. His rage was out of control. I quickly left without them seeing me and asked Daniel to take me back to his house, where it was safe and normal. His family was calm and peaceful.

That was one of the worst memories of my life. My mother stopped seeing that man and my father settled down and continued to deteriorate.

As for me, well, I was still seeing Daniel. I put up with all the flirting that took place whenever women were around. After all, I was only sixteen and he was now twenty-one. That was a big age difference. He was legal and I wasn't. Older, more mature woman wanted him. He might have had other women on the side; I don't know, but I didn't think so. I believe it was all sexual overtures that were brief and fleeting.

I was still going to SAFE at school. We really never learned anything there. I showed up, but that was about it. I got a job at a clothing store, called G&G. I was a sales girl. Since I loved fashion, it was fun.

The manager of the store was this young man who took a liking to me. He was a really good guy. He was one of the only men I knew who never tried to sexually come on to me. Actually, he did his best to help me overcome my low self-esteem, which he had picked up on right away. I guess it wasn't too hard to spot. It probably seemed like I was carrying this huge bag of it over my shoulder, while I thought I was pretty clever in hiding it.

He gave me this book called *How to Be Your Own Best Friend.* He saw the hurt child; he saw the pain in my eyes, and he saw the beautiful soul that I was, too. He was an angel. He was very instrumental in leading me on the path of self-discovery. This was my first book in personal development, a subject I continue to devour to this day. I now had a glimpse into how I could like myself and be good to myself.

---

It was in the spring of 1974 that my father took a turn for the worse. He could no longer work. At the same time, my mom had a very good friend, Roma, who lived across the street. She had three children, Catherine, who was my age; Dianna, who was my brother's age; and an older son, David. David was a savant.

He was extremely bright but he was unable to really carry on a conversation with anyone. He was always calculating numbers in his head while he was walking and talking to himself, and he was a master at chess. I remember playing chess with him one time, and, I am not sure how, but I actually gave him a challenging game. It must have been a fluke, because I was never able to do that again.

Roma thought that she was pregnant. Apparently she had been told by her doctor that she was. But this was not the case at all. She developed some pain, was admitted into the hospital for some tests, and she never left. She had cancer so far advanced that it completely devoured her body. She never even knew what happened. She never regained consciousness after they anesthetized her and opened her up to see what was going on in her uterus. She passed away a few days after that. This happened right before my father's death. My mother was in shock, disbelief, and panic. This happened so fast. My mother's happy thoughts that her friend was having another child soon turned to shock and grief upon hearing of her death. My mom just lost her best friend and was now losing her husband, too.

My father was next to leave this Earth and it happened within the next few days. I was spending most of my time at Daniel's. My father spent most of his time in bed, unable to do much of anything. He was on morphine most of the time but by then it wasn't even helping.

It was the evening of April 21, 1974, one month to the day after his forty-ninth birthday. My mother had to call the ambulance since he was in so much pain. I was lying down, sleeping next to Daniel, when I spontaneously fell out of his bed. I knew right then and there that my father had passed over. I woke up from the fall and said to Daniel, "My father just died." He just held me and comforted me as much as he could. Somehow he knew that this was true.

Shortly after, my mother called me with the news that affirmed this fact. His death was the result of his body becoming septic. All of his pain and suffering that was inside of him, mentally and physically, was able to finally leave. The disintegration of his body would begin; it would go back to where it came from while his soul would go on. Despite what may seem like a tragic event, God's work is always good and everything is for the evolution of mankind.

# CHAPTER 9

After my father was gone, I thought that some sort of peace would reside in my home. But before the light came through, there was more darkness. It was a very difficult time for my mom. I would find her crying often. She just couldn't understand why and how God works. She would scream out, "Why did he have to die? Why do bad people go on, while a good man had to suffer?"

I knew that God didn't make judgments or decide who gets to live or die. I knew that it was about the choices we make, and the thoughts, feelings, and actions we take, that determine the cause and effect in our lives. Like most people, she didn't understand that the relationship between the health in our body, mind, and spirit are all interconnected. I knew that my father was an angry man with a lot of rage and pain. Somehow, I intuitively knew the connection between my father's experiences as a child and his disease. Although I knew all of this, I was a lost soul myself. My mother wasn't able to give me any comfort or answers. My brother was finishing his last year in college, and my father was now gone.

We had a small funeral with a closed casket. He wanted to be cremated and have his ashes spread across the ocean that he'd often traveled back and forth across. I can say that he did have his day in the sun. He got to travel the world, something he absolutely loved. He was able to purchase two apartments in a town called Fuengirola in Costa de Sol, Spain, which was gorgeous. He bought one for himself and one as an investment. He always was smart when it came to money, investments, and opportunities. This was a place that many British and German people traveled to during their winter season. The apartments overlooked the Mediterranean on one side and a mountain range on the other. Maybe in an alternate universe, my father is alive and enjoying his retirement here. It is a nice thought, if nothing else.

—⁓⟡⟡⟡⟡⁓—

After my father's death, we were forced to go on with our lives and pick up the pieces where we could. We had to move forward and learn to live without him. Nadia and Martin were still a part of our lives; however, they were going through a wicked divorce. Nothing stays the same. The bond that seemed so cemented during their youth was being pulled apart in every direction.

Nadia was like a bull in a china shop. I really loved her candid talk; she never held anything back. She would just blurt out whatever was on her mind to anyone. There was no shame in her game. I remember one time, when I was at the farm upstate, she pointed out some pine trees that had been recently planted. There were about six or seven of them. One of them was not doing well and looked as if it was going to die. She said in her thick Russian accent, "You see that tree? Well, that is your father." I was devastated, and I was shocked that she actually said this. Although I knew he was dying, no one dared to verbalize it out loud. Leave it to Nadia to dramatize it. I could never get mad at her, though. I knew her intentions were sincere.

I felt Nadia had some kind of magical abilities where she was able to attract things into her life. She was reacquainted with her father by what seemed like a miracle. Back around 1968, Nadia was attending a Russian play in New York City with a girlfriend. Sitting next to her was an elderly gentleman who had come with a Russian group to see the play. Nadia, being the gregarious woman that she was, struck up a conversation with him. They both quickly realized that they came from the same town in Russia. The gentleman then proceeded to ask what her name was, and she of course said Nadia. He knew immediately that she was his biological daughter and she knew instantaneously that he was her father. What are the chances of reuniting like that after years of being apart, not knowing anything of the other's whereabouts? The war had pulled them apart, but destiny drew them back together. It was an exhilarating moment for the two of them. They remained united until his death on his ninety-second birthday.

———— ∽∾⋏⊙⊙⋎∾∾⋙ ————

After my dad's funeral, when things settled down somewhat, I went back to school and graduated in June of 1974. I have no recollection of the event. I must have been stoned or something—I really do not remember anything from that day.

Daniel and I were still together, but it would not last too much longer. We were invited to a party. It was an older crowd—his friends. I was seventeen and he was twenty-two. I was feeling insecure because of the older, sexy women that were there. I didn't really know anyone and Daniel was off mingling without me. I wanted to just go home but I couldn't find him, so I began searching the rooms looking for him to take me home. All of a sudden the upstairs bathroom door opened; Daniel and some chick came out. That was all that it took for me to have a panic attack. I felt like I'd just gotten punched in the gut. All I could manage to do was to run out of there as fast as I could. Daniel tried to call me back, but I was not having any conversation or explanation. I knew what I saw and I could just imagine what was going on in that small bathroom. I walked back home, alone. I don't remember what I did next—I probably numbed myself with some booze, quaaludes, and pot, and I fell into a deep unconscious state. That was the end of my relationship with Daniel. I knew that if I were to stay with him, I would be hurt often, and that was something I could not bear.

# CHAPTER 10

After breaking up with Daniel, I was in a really depressed state of mind at this time. I didn't know where to turn, what to do, or where to go to get out of my head and my body. Since I was still able to travel with TWA on my father's benefits, I decided to book a trip to San Francisco. I had no plans, I didn't know anyone there, and I didn't have any reservation set up at any hotel. I just wanted to go somewhere, away from anything familiar. My mother wasn't in the frame of mind to stop me, question me, or consider my actions, since she, too, was in a deep depression.

So off I went to California. It was early June of 1974, and I arrived during a massive transportation strike. Of course I was unaware of this ahead of time, so I was at a loss about what to do next. I must have looked like Little Bo Peep who'd lost her sheep. I was standing in the airport crying like a lost soul. A young man came up to me, saying "I wish I could take you home with me, but I wouldn't be able to do that." That was no help, although he did mention going to the YWCA. Ah ha, a destination!

Buses, trolleys, and all mass transportation were on strike. It was crazy. Somehow I got a cab, which was difficult since there was a mad rush for them. I asked the cabby to take me to the YWCA, which he did. I thanked him, paid him the fare, and went inside. I went to the front desk and asked for a room. The person behind the counter told me that they were completely booked up. My heart sank to the ground. I had no idea what I was going to do.

Just then a bubbly, beautiful blonde girl came down the stairs, approaching the front desk to ask them something. She was very vivacious and said hello to me. She asked me my name and where I was from. I told her and mentioned to her my predicament. She said, in a British accent, that she had a room that she was sharing with a friend, and that her friend would be leaving the following evening. If I wanted to, I could take the bed in her room. God is good.

"Yes, yes, I would love to do that!" I said, bursting with joy. All I had to do was find a place to stay for the night. Where to find that place was the question. The Y desk clerk told me of a hotel not too far from there that would probably have rooms available. Since getting another cab was not looking good and there was no other means of transportation, I walked up the hill to the hotel they'd given me the directions to. It wasn't far, but if you've ever been in San Francisco, you know that some of the streets are extremely hilly. Here I was, trudging uphill with a suitcase in hand. Thank God I was so young and in good shape. I managed to make it to this dive, and a dive it was; a pit, a sleazy place that I wouldn't normally dare to step into, but I needed a room and they had one. I locked myself in, afraid to come out until it was daylight. The sounds that echoed through the halls were horrifying. I didn't know if someone was getting raped, murdered, or tortured. I prayed all night long for God to protect me and get me out of there alive. It was a dark, dirty, cold room. And it was a reflection of what was going on inside of me. All the pain and agony that I was feeling was all around me. There was no escape from it. Finally, I was able to fall asleep after pleading with God.

The morning was a welcome sight. There was no delicious sun penetrating into my room, however, since my room had no windows; but I just knew that the sun was there. I couldn't wait to get out of that place. I made a mad dash back to the YWCA to stay with my new best friend. This time it was a much easier, downhill journey, and I knew that I would be OK from this point on.

Things did start to look up. I waited there until Linda came down from her room. True to her word, I was able to stay there for the next few nights. She was a lot of fun to be with. Linda was from South Africa. She was obviously very confident and had good self-esteem. She kind of took me under her wings and invited me everywhere she went. I loved her energy. Everything was light and easygoing around her. She laughed with the rhythms of the day. It was just what I needed to relieve my heavy heart.

Linda was another angel who came into my life. It never ceases to amaze me, the angels who appear just when you need them the most. I always have faith that things will work out even when it seems that the darkness is so thick. After the few days were over, I was able to get in touch with some relatives of my mother, Annalisa and Gunther, who lived in San Luis Obispo, California. This is about a six- or seven-hour car ride from San Francisco. The buses were up and running by that time, so I was able to visit them. They are a wonderful couple, both doctors, around fifty years old at the time. They practiced the Baha'i faith, and still do. I had only met them a couple of times before, but they were so kind and gentle and always had an open door for anyone that needed a place to stay. Not only did I need a bed to sleep in, but I was most certainly in need of spiritual healing as well.

When I arrived at their home, I was graciously accepted and warmed by their genuine spirit. I immediately felt relieved to be somewhere comforting and nurturing. For the next week and a half I was able to connect with my higher self. Annalisa and Gunther guided me back home, into my essence. They held spiritual gatherings in their home, where I felt safe. Through their practice, readings, and discussions, I understood what it felt like to be connected to God. They showed me who I really am; Pure love, pure bliss, and pure peace. It was a feeling I wanted more of.

I cried when I had to leave. A part of me wanted to stay there. I wanted to keep that feeling forever. How could I remain in that state of being as I went back to New York, and back to the world that had caused me so much pain? These lovely people were so normal compared to what I was used to. How did my parents get so messed up? Annalisa and Gunther also both came from Germany, although they came here at a much younger age than my parents had, and weren't Jewish. Annalisa had lost both her parents in the war; they had died together in their home when it was bombed by the Americans. She said the funny thing was that her parents had been born on the same day and year, and died on the same day, too. Coincidence? I don't think so. It seemed to me there was a bond between them that was destined to be connected on many planes of consciousness. Annalisa was probably a teenager when she arrived in the States. Her husband Gunther came here about the same time and they met in California, where they have lived ever since.

When the time came, I left the confines of their sanctuary and headed home. I felt the sadness begin to creep back into my bones on the plane ride to for New York.

# CHAPTER 11

After my summer in California, I was finished with school and needed to find employment. College was not an option I had considered. I'd had various jobs while I was in high school: the clothing store; babysitting here and there; and in a factory, where I made knishes and egg rolls for some company. I had also worked down the block from my home making amplifiers and accessories for guitars. There were a couple of guys who owned this business and they only hired good looking girls to work there. It was kind of funny; we all knew that if you got hired there that you were a hottie.

Now I was approaching eighteen and I needed to buy a car, find a job, and begin to live my life as an adult. I bought my first car, a red Ford Pinto. I thought it was great. I got a job in a diner. (Hmm, do you see any connection here?) The town I worked in, back in the late '70s was full of mental patients who were placed in old hotels that were once beautiful places. Now they were run-down and pretty decrepit. Many of these unstable people would frequent our diner. Some of them worked there, too. They were harmless; but totally crazy. The medications they were taking probably made them that way. I don't believe they received any therapy, only prescriptions. Some of these people had been functioning members of society at one time, but life had thrown them some curve balls and they didn't have the support or the know-how to pick themselves back up.

I enjoyed working at the diner, though. I like being around people and talking to them. To me it is so fascinating to discover who people are and to listen to their stories. We all have stories inside of us.

Life was beginning to settle down and I was finding some joy in my journey through life. Daniel was calling me in the hopes that we would be able to reconnect. I was sure tempted, but I knew better. I didn't want to feel that pain again. Anyway, there was another guy, Frank, who was pursuing me. He saw me play tennis with a friend one day, and was smitten by my hot little body. He approached me on the tennis courts; I really wasn't interested in him, or anyone else for that matter. I just wanted to be normal and be happy with myself.

But Frank was very persuasive. He would not leave me alone. He left notes on my car, then flowers, and then started hanging around wherever I was. I eventually broke down and went out with him. He was a very passionate guy, but he had no direction. He was delusional about being this godlike figure. He really thought that he was some kind of gorgeous, wonderful guy that any and all girls would be madly in love with. Well, he did manage to persuade one vulnerable, naive young girl—me. I gave in. I could not stand the onslaught of his daily stalking. Before you knew it, we were together.

Daniel was still calling me and practically begging me to get back together with him. I was so torn. I really loved Daniel, and I never really loved Frank. The turning point came when I was on the phone with Daniel—he was trying to convince me just to see him so that we could talk in person—while Frank was in the room with me, pulling me away from the phone and telling me to hang up. I was so confused I didn't know what to do. Finally I told Daniel no and that was the end.

I was hitched to Frank. He got what he wanted and I got a guy I didn't love. I grew to like him and we had some good times together; however, he was not someone I would have chosen if I were in a stronger state of mind. He was controlling and manipulative and I was becoming weaker, more introverted, and more docile. He came from a very Catholic Italian family where the man of the house is the king and the woman is the worker bee. Sure enough, I would take over this role and perfect it. We continued to live on Long Island for the next few years. He moved into my house, which my mother was not too happy about, but Frank just did what he wanted without asking for permission. My mom got a job as an inspector at a coat factory. She loved her job. She was among like-minded people, being useful, and working hard. She didn't get paid nearly what she was worth, but she never complained and never asked for more. Her self-worth was never encouraged, so she thought that woman should just settle for what they got and be happy about it. She was definitely not a feminist.

My mom did not like Frank very much. She had really liked Daniel, and so had my dad, surprisingly enough. I know my father would not have liked Frank at all. If he were alive there would have been no chance in hell that Frank would have been in my life. It was not the wisest decision to have stayed with Frank; however, it was the choice I made and it has taught me many things about myself that I am thankful for.

We all have many choices that determine the direction of our life. It is so important to be aware of what we really want and decide with our hearts if that choice is going to move us closer to that outcome. If we feel the slightest doubt, we need to honor that feeling and step back from making a decision that could potentially alter the course of our lives forever. Our intuition is always speaking to us in quiet whispers, and we need to learn how to be still and to listen to these messages that God is giving us.

There were many red flags that popped up about the choices I was making. I ignored them all, thinking I was able to control the path of my life. Frank and I were very much into music and we went to see many concerts in the city with various friends. We liked to trip out on LSD while we were at these concerts, since it enhanced our auditory faculties. We felt that we became one with the music. It was awesome. We saw Santana, The Crusaders, Led Zeppelin, and many more all while under the influence of LSD and other narcotics. Frank started developing a cocaine habit at this time. He had two older brothers, one of whom started dealing the stuff. I never really liked cocaine, but I went along with the crowd and used it, too. It made me wired, but I was already wired, so I didn't need much before I was bouncing off the walls. Frank really liked it and so did our friends. Drugs seemed to be everywhere. I knew a few kids who got involved with heroin while we were still in high school. That drug really scared me and I never got into using needles. LSD, mescaline, cocaine, marijuana, Quaaludes, alcohol—these were my preferred drugs. Though I could say I had my fair share of substance abuse, I never got addicted to any.

Frank got a job working for his brother, Paddy, who owned a printing shop in upstate New York. Paddy needed help so it was easy for Frank to begin work there. The commute was way too long from Long Island and we decided to move up there. We found a nice cottage-like house to rent nearby, about a half an hour away from his job. It was a great place, right next to a nature preserve. I really enjoyed this, and it reminded me of being on Martin and Nadia's farm. But I became very reclusive since I was so far away from anyone I knew, and people in general for that matter. At the time, we only had one car; I had sold my Pinto before we left to move up there. Frank had a green 1965 Mustang. It was a really cool car. He used it to go to work, so I was left home alone.

I became very attached to Frank and he became my center, my world. I think that is exactly how he wanted it. I started to become very restless and needed to do more, though. I felt like I was being brainwashed or something, so I told him that we needed to buy another car—which we did. Thank God, I was now able to travel about and do things. I became very close to Maria, Frank's brother's wife. We had a good bond and we visited them often. They lived about an hour away, and had two cute little boys. Since Paddy was dealing drugs, he always had money and nice things. They had a pool on their property that we used often in the summer. I always felt like an outsider around them, though. I never felt like I belonged—maybe because I really didn't belong there.

My intuition was letting me know that something more was waiting for me. I just didn't know what or where, or how to go about getting it. As the saying goes, if you don't have a plan, you plan to fail. If you don't have a vision for your life, you will flounder, and that is exactly what seemed to be happening. Somehow I knew I needed to move forward, to get involved in outside activities. But what? That was the big question.

———⟊⟊————

Maria had mentioned to me that the school where she did some volunteer work needed a dance instructor. Since I was an excellent dancer and had always taken some sort of class in ballet, modern, or jazz, I thought this would be a great opportunity for me. I was in excellent shape, so I applied for the position and I got it. It was an after-school dance program for little girls, ages five to ten.

I taught ballet. It was harder than I'd expected. Children that young do not listen well unless you really know how to engage them. Sometimes I did; other times, not so much. I had migraines after each class. I finished out the year, but did not sign up to do it again. I was definitely not ready for that and I didn't like it.

I was turning twenty and Frank wanted to get married. I didn't. Of course like everything else I did with him, he persuaded me to do it. I was not ready for marriage, at least not with him. I didn't love him and I knew it. He had a best friend named Adam, whom I started liking. During our drug-induced parties Adam and I would wind up finding each other very attractive. Little by little we began having an affair. Looking back I believe it was my way out of my life with Frank—I sabotaged our relationship by having this affair. Here was my saboteur archetype appearing. This one was a biggie for me. I would sabotage myself often until I became aware of it. But Frank didn't find out until later, and I went through the motions of getting married to him. We had a big wedding, which my mother paid for. We found an old mansion in Connecticut, a beautiful castle-like home, to host the reception. I did not wear a traditional wedding dress. I didn't want to. It was off-white and simple. We had a great live jazz band. At least he and I agreed about good music. We also had a ton of cocaine at the wedding. Because of this, I don't remember much of anything. I had only two tables of friends from my mother's side while the rest were all Frank's family and friends. Nadia and Martin did not come. Michael and his fiancé, Steven and a few other family friends attended. Maria was my maid of honor, and I had no bridesmaids. We had a golden retriever, Sierra, who was part of the wedding ceremony, too. The band was enjoying the mound of cocaine that Paddy had supplied as a wedding gift. It was a crazy time. Adam was Frank's best man. What a sham this all was, celebrating a marriage I knew wasn't going to work out. I just didn't have the backbone to come out and say it. I didn't think; how could I? I had too many drugs floating around my brain and warping my thinking. I didn't like who I was becoming, that I know, and I knew I needed to make some changes.

All of us are born with the ability to differentiate between right and wrong, and with the ability to achieve. But some of us must run head-on into a stone wall, and smash ourselves to bits and pieces before we really know what it's all about. I had to hit the wall with a terrific crash a few times before I would transform and begin understanding the laws of the universe.

———✳———

After all the hoopla of the wedding was over, we left for a honeymoon in Mexico. That was going to be interesting, because by this time I was not interested in having sex with my new husband anymore. I was hot for his best friend. How was I going to get out of this one? What was supposed to be a joyous occasion ended up being a nightmare. Somehow Frank and Adam had set it up that we were to meet in Florida after the honeymoon. We were going to fly into Florida, meet Adam, who'd scored a ton of pot down there, and we all were going to drive home together. Great plan, don't you think?

So there we were, in Mexico, and it was scorching hot. The first day we were there, we had plans to go out in a small boat. I put my bathing suit on, dabbed some suntan lotion on and off we went. I love the sun and the heat; however, my body was not anywhere near ready for the intense sun that beat down on me. I got third-degree burns all over my body. Ouch! I was hurting bad. No one could touch me. Well, there was my way out from having sex with Frank on my honeymoon. Brilliant.

My subconscious mind was much more powerful than I gave it credit for. I put the intention out there and sure enough my subconscious found a way. Never underestimate the power of intention. Negative or positive, it will respond. You will get what you ask for—though not always in the way you had expected. This is why it is so important to be specific. The more you can consciously focus on what you want and hold that intention, the more it can and will manifest into physical form. I was learning this through the years, although it took me a long time to really grasp it and integrate it into my life. I didn't think for myself at this young age; I succumbed to the suggestion of others. I easily gave my power away; thank God I had a tremendous supply of it. I was a feisty one. I was born with a huge zest to live. I just needed to learn how to stay in my power, and distribute it as I desired.

———— ᜁᜁᜁᜁ ————

The rest of our honeymoon was ruined. I was indoors and in bed, moving as little as possible. Frank was not too happy about this, but that's what I wanted. I didn't want to be in so much pain, but that's what I got, because I wasn't specific enough. The day came when we had to fly to Florida and meet Adam, who was waiting for us with a carload of marijuana. It all went smoothly. He picked us up at the Miami airport and we got a hotel room for the evening with plans to drive to New York the next day. I was feeling better and able to make the trip without too much discomfort.

Adam and I wanted to be with each other and we often exchanged glances and what I called mental thought waves of lust. We both felt it intensely. Frank was oblivious to the romance that was taking place right under his nose. Maybe he trusted us, or maybe his ego was so large that he thought we wouldn't dare do anything like this to him. It was a morally despicable act of betrayal. If I knew better, I would have done better. Being dishonest and disloyal is never right. My behavior was immature and pitiful. At the time, I didn't think that way. I was guided by my emotions, and my conscious mind was on hiatus. We arrived home in Westchester, where we were now living, without a hitch. Everything went smoothly and I guess they sold all the pot. That wasn't my department, and I didn't want to know.

Adam would stay over a lot, and during the days when Frank went to work, Adam and I would make love. It felt good, maybe because I was being rebellious, or maybe because Adam was my choice, I don't know, but I was the one who had initiated the affair and I was the one who could put a stop to it if I wanted to. As much I relinquished my will to Frank, I found a way to get it back with Adam. As I said, this was the coward's way out, but it was the only way I knew how to operate at the time. I just didn't have all the tools. No one had taught them to me. In my heart I knew it was wrong, but I suppressed this feeling to my utmost ability.

After adjusting to married life, we moved a little further northwest, to Duchess County. I didn't particularly like the house we were in. It was rather plain and didn't have much character. My home space was important to me. I liked to personalize the spaces in order to make them mine. This place just felt cold from the get-go. As I mentioned at the beginning of this story, I believe places hold energy. The walls retain the vibrations of all those who have been there before. This place had a strange energy, and I felt a negative pull.

I started going to night school for horticulture through the Cornell Extension Program. I loved it, and for once, I was very dedicated to my studies. It was very extensive and the course was an in-depth study of all aspects of the plant world. During the day, I got a job as a server during the morning shift at a place called Wilma's. (See the pattern repeat again and again.) It was more than just a diner. During the morning and afternoon it was a luncheonette, but three nights a week they were open for dinner. The owner was a gourmet chef and his wife ran the business affairs. It was a very friendly place, and I really enjoyed working there. I met so many wonderful people and made many connections. It was at this time that I was beginning to spread my wings and learn how to fly.

Frank and I decided to find a mate for our golden retriever, and began researching possible candidates. We found a beautiful male with a reddish fur. About two months later Sierra had ten puppies. Ten puppies, wow! It was a lot of work, and of course I did most of it. I have to say, I did enjoy tending to those little guys. We sold all of them but one, whom we kept and named Nabisco. He was a terror. Not anything like his mother, who was calm, obedient, and smart. Nabisco was crazy. He was always getting into something. When I would come home from work, you would find things torn apart and garbage all over the house. He was full of mischief.

About this time, I got word that my grandma Betty (my father's mother) had passed. She had spent her last years in a nursing home in Zurich, Switzerland. The last time I'd gone to see her was a few years before then, in London. She was beginning to lose her memory and was becoming very paranoid. She thought people were always coming into the apartment and stealing things. The last visit I had with her, she hid my passport and told me someone had come in and stolen it. I had to make a trip to the embassy to get a temporary one to fly back home, but when I arrived back at her apartment, she had somehow found it. We were unable to fly over for her funeral, but I received a few thousand dollars' in an inheritance from her. I was also receiving another few thousand dollars from my father's will, since I was now twenty-one.

I wanted to buy a home. I had always wanted to have my own place and now was the perfect opportunity. I started scouting out homes and land. I came across an older home in upper Westchester that I loved. It needed work but sat on over twenty acres of land. I had a good eye for real estate and instinctively knew that it was a good deal. I thought that we could live in the house, even though it needed work, and hold on to the property. My mom was totally against it and was not supportive. This was shortly before I'd turned twenty-one. She was the guardian of the money that was left to me until I became of age, and she would not relinquish the funds for the property. Today it is probably worth millions of dollars. So, on to the next.

I met a woman at Wilma's, the restaurant I was working at, and became very good friends with her. She was a real estate agent. She showed us several houses, one of which I would buy. It was a small but lovely two-bedroom home, in great shape, which was located in Connecticut. There were three acres of land and a long, expansive driveway. We purchased the house for $52,000. In today's market the house would be worth at least $800,000, if not more.

It was the first place I could call mine. Everything seemed to be going well. I was working at the restaurant during the day, going to horticultural school at night, and in between, taking care of Frank, the house, and the dogs. Adam would come up every so often, or we would visit friends down on Long Island, where he lived. Something, however, was gnawing at my spirit. It didn't feel good living a lie. I became restless for change and knew something would have to happen. I knew that a sabotage event would have to be created to stir things up, and a perfect scene was about to reveal itself. Frank came home early from work one day. I asked him what he was doing home so early and he said that he had a fight with his brother and that he wasn't going back any more. So all the burden of paying the mortgage and everything else would be on me. Not to mention I was cutting the acres of lawn, cooking, cleaning, shopping, and more. I did it all. I allowed myself to be the workhorse. It was crazy, but that is how I sought approval from others. My self-worth was based on proving myself worthy by always giving things away and doing as much as I could.

Once, when I was on the tractor cutting the lawn, I fell backward over the retaining driveway wall while I was still sitting on the mower. It was about a three-foot drop. I managed to use what felt like super-human strength to get the tractor off my leg. When I turned off the engine and assessed the damage to my body, I saw my left thigh swelling up and a round burn from the muffler embedded in my thigh. I felt no pain since I was in shock. No one was home and it was a distance to the next house in the area. I got in my '65 Ford Mustang and drove to my friend's house, a few houses down. When I rang the bell she was happy but surprised to see me. Then she looked down and saw my leg, and was shocked at how swollen it was. She took me to the hospital right away. After some x-rays and tests, they released me. I had a hematoma that would take several weeks to heal and a badly sprained coccyx, but no broken bones or other injuries. I was very lucky. I still have the scar of the muffler burn on my thigh.

Anyway, Frank was home from work and I was not happy with him being home all day while I was practically running myself ragged. Things started heating up between us. I was getting my mojo back to speak my mind. He did not like me having such a strong opinion about things. I joined an environmental group at this time called People for Safe Energy. I was learning so much about plants and the environment. I began reading books on cosmology, earth science, and energy sources. I read Rachael Carlson's book, *Silent Spring*, which should be required reading for everyone on this planet. I was waking up, discovering myself more and more, and loving it.

In the midst of all this, I discovered that I was pregnant—and Adam was the father. I never told anyone about it, and sought a doctor to give me an abortion. Abortions were legal then. I couldn't believe that it happened. I just felt that I couldn't have the baby. It would have been too complicated. So here I was, reliving my mother's anguish over having an abortion. This time it was my decision, and I went through with terminating the pregnancy. In a way, I felt like I was trying to kill a part of me, like some cellular memory that knew I could have been aborted. Actually, that was why I was often so self-destructive. I knew that I was unwanted, and a part of me wanted to kill myself. I recovered very quickly from the procedure, although my hormones were a mess.

———— ∿•◦◦⊙◦⊙◦◦•∿ ————

When I had healed from the procedure and the accident, I started working at another place. Hey, what's another job, with all that I was doing? I was working for a guy who was starting a garden center. That is where I met this woman, Dina. She was about ten years older than me and very trippy. I gravitated to eccentric people and they latched on to me as well. We quickly became friends. Her parents were living on Long Island. Coincidence? No way! Dina grew up in Europe. She went to boarding schools and spoke French and Italian fluently. Her parents had owned an American-style restaurant in Italy, which supposedly had been a big hit. Half of what Dina told me seemed so far-fetched I wasn't sure if it was real or imagined. I think she'd done one too many hits of acid. She said that in Italy, she had been friends with a lot of popular musicians of the times, and they would come into the restaurant. I'm sure some of it was real. Her parents, who were eccentric, too, verified the star-studded stories when I visited them on Long Island.

To me it was all very fascinating. I loved exotic people. I got bored with the ordinary. As Dina and I were getting closer, her independent influence was rubbing off on me. You see, you become who you associate with; that's why it is so important to surround yourself with people who are going somewhere. People with a purpose and vision. People who have goals and are positive-minded. I had an eclectic group of friends. I liked to keep things interesting. Dina didn't have goals or a vision; however, she did help me see that I needed to grow, and staying in this relationship with Frank was not going to allow me do that.

Frank did not like Dina at all. He refused to have her at our house. He didn't like that she was so outspoken, and thought she was putting ideas into my head—which she was. She threatened his manhood, or should I say macho-hood. Things started to get so out of control and it was then that I decided to leave and stay at my mother's house. He started to put demands on me and issue repercussions, like if I wasn't home at a certain time I wouldn't be allowed to go out with Dina. He tried to stop me from going back to my mom's, but when my mind is made, that's it. This was the beginning of the end of our marriage. It was also the end of Adam. Frank began having an affair with some girl he met. He was living in the house and I moved back to my mother's house. I slept on the living room sofa. My mom had moved into the basement apartment since she was alone. She thought she didn't need so much room and rented out the two upper units. It was a small, dark, crammed apartment. I hated it. I got so depressed there. My mom never had a knack for decorating. Her places never felt warm or cozy. Most of the time I would stay in bed and just feel sorry for myself. I was such a good victim.

I needed to get out of there. I convinced my mom to take back the second floor unit so that I could at least have a bedroom and some natural light. Somehow that happened rather quickly. I was only twenty-one, yet felt like I'd experienced so much. Marriage, an affair, a house, and now a separation and pending divorce. I retained an attorney to proceed with the legalities. He was not an aggressive or even an assertive lawyer. Things dragged on for some time. Frank was living in the house that we purchased with the money I'd received from my inheritance, and I was living back home with my mom. Something did not add up. However, I was happy to be free. I had the two dogs, Sierra and Nabisco, at the time. I really took much better care of them than Frank had. But Frank's goal was to strip me of everything, and he arrived at my mom's house with an officer and a court order to take the dogs back with him. I'm not sure how that went down, but he did manage to leave with them and I was left heartbroken.

# Chapter 12

My divorce was a big turning point for me. I wanted to run away and experience something new.

My next stops were Australia, New Zealand, Hawaii, and California again. I was adventurous, and since I had some relatives in Sydney, I thought this would be a good opportunity to visit them and see the bottom half of the earth. I left right after Christmas and I planned to be away for the entire winter. At least I had somewhat of a plan this time, rather than just wandering on a plane not knowing anyone or where to stay. Plans are good. Even though in my heart of hearts I know everything will work out in the end, it's always good to have some kind of a plan.

Off I went, by myself, to Sydney. I arrived about a day later in Australia. Fred, my second cousin from my father's side, picked me up. He lived in one of the most desirable locations in Sydney, Bondi Beach. It was the beginning of their summer and it was warm and delicious. I love the sun.

Fred was married to a woman named Denise who kept a kosher house. They did not have a harmonious marriage. Fred had a fraternal twin, David, whose wife's name was Sahara. They seemed happier with each other. Lenny, their younger brother, still lived at home with their mom, dad, and grandmother, also in Bondi Beach. Their grandma from their mom's side had been in Auschwitz. She had the numbers tattooed on her arm. She and her sister were very young when they were in the camps, so she didn't remember many stories, but you could see them all in her eyes. Her eyes revealed the holocaust. They were these hollow, dark mirrors that showed the terror, fear, and pain that they must have witnessed, all the while not knowing of their fate. Yet she was a very sweet lady.

---

I made myself at home there in Bondi Beach. It was a relaxing, no-worry atmosphere, which was exactly what I needed. I had been so tense back in New York. Because of my level of anxiety, I'd stopped menstruating. My body went into fight or flight mode. You would think I was in adrenaline failure, but just the opposite. I had tons of energy. Female athletes are known to stop their menses if they are training hard. What your body does is reserve the energy for survival and the task at hand while halting any unnecessary function. I find our bodies absolute miracles. I am in awe over how our mind, body, and spirit are all intertwined.

Even though things were much calmer down under, my mind knew there were things back home that were unresolved. Our subconscious keeps tabs on everything. All those stored programs and archetypes are ready to pop up at any time if one's conscious mind is not in the present moment and aware of what's going on.

---

Lenny and a male friend were planning to travel by car up to Cairns, the northernmost part of Australia's east coast. They asked me if I wanted to come along. I was in. We were going to be camping out, pitching a tent at night and traveling by day. Little did I know about the rough Australian men. This was not what I was used to at all. It started out all right. The first few nights were uneventful. But soon they were acting thick-headed, macho, and stupid. They just wouldn't listen to anything I had to say.

We arrived at some friends of Lenny's in Queensland, about halfway to Cairns.

There were some other young people there, too, including two girls, one from Germany and another from Sweden, both named Karen. Now what are the chances of having three Karens in one place? We stayed there two nights and had a good time. The weather was superb and getting hotter, since we were getting closer to the equator.

We said our goodbyes and continued our journey. That was where it got really interesting. During the day, the drive was very monotonous, with rubber trees lining the way on both sides. There was only one lane in each direction. Back in the late 1970s not many people traveled these roads. The twisting and turning of the dead trees along the way took on the appearance of various shapes and beings. My LSD days had left me with a good imagination. At night, there were no lights to illuminate the roads. The stars were some of the brightest I've ever had the privilege of seeing. It appeared as if the heavens were going to burst open before me. There were no artificial lights anywhere in sight to obscure the view. I could see how the aborigines, or any indigenous tribe, were so connected to the Earth.

As we were driving along on this pitch-black night, Lenny's friend, who was driving, spotted hitchhiker number one. He stopped to pick a woman up. First of all, I was shocked that anyone would be out here in the night looking for a ride. You couldn't see anything. She was stoned or drunk and said in an Aussie drawl that she'd just left her boyfriend. She started babbling on about what an ass he was. Blah, blah, blah. I was sitting in the back with her and I was not thrilled. Again, like a ghost in the night, hitchhiker number two appeared. I didn't know if it was a common thing that people just randomly walked to the edge of the road in the night looking for rides, but I thought it odd. This time it was a drunk old man. He kept on falling asleep and leaning on me. I had enough of all this and we dropped them off about an hour down the road at some joint. The bars that they had were like the old western saloons. All you saw were men in them; women could go in, but you never saw many. When I walked in, heads turned. I didn't like the scene at all. We got back on the road and drove for a couple more hours. We finally stopped the car and were ready to set up camp. Because it was so late and dark, I did not feel comfortable setting up the tent not knowing the lay of the land. I decided to sleep in the car. Lenny and his buddy slept in the tent. The sun rose early and it was hot as soon as the sun touched the horizon, around 6:00 a.m. I woke up being bothered by something biting me. It was ants. Ants were everywhere. I quickly got out of the car and woke up Lenny. He saw that they had built their tent on an ant hill. Ouch! Lenny's friend was still fast asleep, not fazed by them. I don't know how that could be, but some Australian men are just so stoic, he being one of them.

Lenny and I took the car for a fast drive to get the ants off the outside of the hood, since they were covering the car. They weren't red ants, thank God, but they were definitely bad enough. When we got back, Mr. Macho was awake and pretty bitten up. I hoped they learned the lesson of setting up the tent while there was still enough light to see where they were and what they were doing.

We finally arrived in Cairns; it was a beautiful tropical paradise. There were lakes and waterfalls, lots of sun, and a myriad of vegetation and animal life. There were giant toads, bugs, and spiders—it seemed like everything was huge here. We swam in the beautiful waters of the Great Barrier Reef, and visited an old rainforest just north of Cairns. The primeval landscape was magical. Back then, not many people ventured to this location, so we pretty much had the place to ourselves.

We had an opportunity to board a sailboat and sail to a deserted island off the main coast. The boat crew dropped us off—they would return in two days to pick us up. There were no hotels, inns, or any accommodations. Visitors had to bring their own sleeping bags, food, water and supplies. It was like being Tom Hanks in *Cast Away*. The island had a huge supply of mango trees, and I had mangos for breakfast, lunch, and dinner. I didn't mind it. I love mangos, and what could be better than ripe, freshly picked ones? I love adventures like these, and it brought me back to my days at the farm when I was the pioneer woman in the treehouse. I was a survivor and knew how to get by with very little. The island was quite barren so there wasn't much to do but to stay close to shore, swim near the Barrier Reef, and explore the beautiful coral. We did some exploration; however, as I mentioned earlier, the insect world was rather large here and I didn't want to run into any unexpected visitors that could bite! After the two days were up, the boat picked us up and back we went to the mainland.

We contemplated traveling across the waters to Papua, New Guinea. It wasn't too far away, but we'd heard some crazy stories about the indigenous tribes doing some head hunting and we didn't want to be scalped, so we decided against it. We headed back to Sydney and arrived a few days later.

After resting, back at Cousin Fred's house, we all planned another trip to Jindabyne, southwest of Sydney. It was near Mount Kosciuszko, which is one of the only skiing areas in Australia. It wasn't skiing season; we went for the scenery. There were a few of us on this trip: Fred, his wife, his wife's two sisters, Lenny, and myself. We rented some cabins there to spend the night, and then looked for a place to have dinner. We came across a restaurant called the Austrian Loft. It was a quaint, cozy place with Austrian fare.

A gentleman named Ganter Beliz owned the place and was also the chef. He was from Austria. There was a small German and Austrian influence there, and Ganter and I immediately made a connection. Since I spoke German, we were able to communicate in the language he was most comfortable with. After finishing our dinner, he asked if he could meet me the next day. I agreed and came to the restaurant the next afternoon. We talked and found a common ground. He had two children from a previous marriage, whom he was raising. His ex-wife was living back in Sydney with her new husband. Samantha, his daughter, was stunningly beautiful. She had dark skin, with long, straight, jet-black hair. Her features were strikingly sharp and angular and she was tall and lean. Ganter was not her biological father, but had wanted to raise her anyway. He and his ex-wife had gone to Papua, New Guinea, for their honeymoon. Her father was some kind of diplomat there, so they got special perks. She met a native man there, had sex with him and became pregnant, but never told Ganter about it. When Samantha was born nine months later, he got the message and figured things out. His ex was a tall, beautiful blonde. Their son Kenny, who was a few years younger, was his natural son. He said he was never angry over this and loved them both equally. I could see that this was true. These are the tangled webs we weave, when we are not thinking of the consequences to our actions. There is a law of physics, of cause and effect, which, if not adhered to, will deliver unwanted results. When we are young, hormonally driven, and not grounded, it will tempt us to deviate from the path of truth. We hurt others, punish ourselves, and suffer the consequences.

Ganter was looking for a wife, mother, and waitress all in one woman. Guess who I became? I had found a new home, Jindabyne. I moved into Ganter's house and played mother, wife, and waitress at the Austrian Loft. It was fun for about four weeks, until I started getting restless. I was thousands of miles away from anything remotely familiar. My family had gone back to Sydney, where they had jobs and everyday responsibilities. I stayed, taking on my new role.

Nothing was convenient here. Even the nearest shopping center for food was at least an hour's drive away. What on earth was I thinking? I wasn't—that's the thing. I was being led by hormones and sex. Ganter wanted to marry me. Really? After four weeks?

I wrote and called my mom and a girlfriend back home. They both pleaded with me to come back home. They thought I was crazy if I decided to stay there. I really didn't want to, but I was confused. It was now the beginning of March. Time seemed to have drifted, and I was finding it more and more difficult to make a decision.

I finally told Ganter that I needed to go back to Sydney, see my relatives, and pick up the rest of my belongings. I flew back on a small commuter plane. Back at Fred's I felt a sigh of relief. The feeling of pressure from a man when he wants you to commit to something you aren't ready for is extremely uncomfortable. I knew I couldn't and wouldn't marry Ganter. I was too young, Jindabyne was too isolated, and I definitely wasn't ready for children.

I stayed in Sydney for another two weeks before heading out to New Zealand. Ganter was very upset over this. I told him I needed to get back to the States because I had to finalize my divorce, which was true. I didn't have the chutzpa to totally be honest with him, to say, "Ganter, I really like you a lot and think you are an incredible man, father, and cook; however, I am not the woman for you. I do not want to be your wife, mother of your children, or server." No, I just took the path of least resistance. But I was free again, and it felt good.

Next stop: Auckland, New Zealand. I was in awe from the moment I landed. I never saw a more beautiful, lush, green place! It seemed that I had gone back in time at least a hundred years. I booked myself on a tour and stayed with a small group of very nice people. They were an eclectic mix from different parts of the world. I thoroughly enjoyed my time in New Zealand. The landscape was so rich with natural beauty that it took my breath away ... no ... actually, it did the opposite. It offered me a space to breathe more deeply, as I took in all the splendor the land had to offer.

I went to geothermal springs and soaked in natural sulfur baths. There were redwood trees that grew to majestic heights in a quarter of the time it took for similar trees to grow in California, because of the soil being so fertile in New Zealand. Everyone I encountered there was warm and friendly. There was a calming vibe to the land. Unfortunately, it was time to leave and continue on my way.

───── ✴ ─────

My next stop was Hawaii. Guess who was living there now? None other than my first true love, Daniel. Did I look him up? You bet I did. He was living on the main Island of Waikiki. I was surprised to discover that Waikiki was a big city. It had skyscrapers and lots of large hotels, and the beaches were packed with tourists. Of course it wasn't anywhere near the size of New York; however, I wasn't expecting this. I am sure the other islands were not as developed as this one, but because of my time frame, I was not able to venture off to the other islands.

I called Daniel up and he was very nice, and was happy to hear from me. He picked me up and invited me to his home. He was married and I got to meet his wife. She was not so happy to see me. Could I blame her? Really, an old flame resurfacing for no reason other than to say hello? I didn't want to create any havoc between them so I thought it best to leave. It didn't seem like there was love between them. I got the vibe that their marriage would not last. I was right. They eventually did divorce. You can pick up on the energy of people and places if you are in tune with them. I was always able to sense this. I was so disappointed about Daniel being in a loveless marriage.

Back in my hotel room, I pondered what to do next. A floodgate of memories opened up. They poured into my conscious mind and I became sad and lonely. When my thoughts lead me astray, I abuse myself. Trouble was on the horizon. As night approached, I got dressed in something revealing and headed down to a local nightclub. I wanted to numb myself of the pain that was circulating through my mind and body, so I had a few drinks. It doesn't take many to get me drunk. There was a big black male who was the bouncer at the door. He laid eyes on me as I came in and he noticed me inside getting inebriated. Being the nice guy that he was, he offered to take me back to my hotel room. I didn't put up much of an argument, and I was off, back to my hotel room. The big, nice guy turned into a big, not-so-nice rapist. He had his way with me and I was in no condition to put up a fight. The next morning, I felt awful. Not only did I have a wicked hangover, I felt violated, depressed, and downright horrible. I wanted out. I shoved all my depressed feelings down into the pit of my gut, as I had always done, and went on my way.

Soon I was back on a plane. Next stop: Los Angeles. Friends of my father lived there, and they had a daughter around my age. They were very conservative, which was exactly the frame of mind I needed right then to set me straight and get my head in some kind of order. I put what happened behind me as best I could. Either that or I sucked it in, which is also something I was good at doing. I've learned that when you do not honestly confront yourself, and try to cover things up, it only gets worse. What you resist will persist, as Deepak Chopra says. That is why I believe the things that happened to me that appeared bad were only things coming to the surface in order to be healed. But I still needed to get knocked down a few more times before I would surrender to myself.

---

I stayed in L.A. for a few days. It was an uneventful time with no drama. This bored me. I was addicted to drama. I needed some chaos to keep things interesting. Anyway, I needed to get back to New York to finalize my divorce. I knew it was going to be coming up soon, since I had been away for months. While on the plane ride home, I met a guy who took one look at me and seduced me. I had sex with him on the plane. I wasn't a sex addict, although you would think I was. I was just a lonely, confused, mixed-up young girl. I could see how Marilyn Monroe must have felt. Her life was like this times a hundred. She was so beautiful, yet so lonely and vulnerable. "Like a candle in the wind, never knowing who to cling to when the rain set in," as the song goes. That was how I felt.

After we landed, we said our goodbyes and back to Long Island it was.

# CHAPTER 13

It was now April. I thought I would beat the winter, but we happened to have a freak snowstorm a week after I had returned. I was not too happy to see snow. I am a sun worshiper and cold weather and I do not do well together. Thank God, it warmed up shortly after that.

Soon after, I received a call from the attorney saying that I needed to come up to the courthouse in Connecticut to finalize the divorce proceedings. It was a cut-and-dry divorce. He would get the house and I got about $3,000.00. I didn't put up a fight; I just wanted it to be over so that I could get on with my life. These things that are unsettled hold you back mentally, physically, and spiritually. The day after I signed the divorce papers, I finally got my period. I couldn't believe how intelligent my body was. It knew when to surrender. It knew it was time to let go. I was able to close the door on that part of my life and begin a whole new set of experiences. That is exactly what I did.

I was now twenty-three and I was cruising for a bruising. Being the hot, sexy lady that I was, I got jobs as a cocktail waitress. I worked at various different bars and clubs. This one bar where a friend I knew, who is now dead from a cocaine overdose, was the bartender. He was always high on something. I don't know how he even worked, since he was always slurring his words and half in the bag. One night when I had offered to give him a ride home, a sleazy-looking character approached him, at my car. It was probably about 3:00 AM and he wasn't too happy. He was twisting some sort of wire in his hands and asking Steve, my friend, to give him what he owed him. Steve kept on telling him in his slurred speech that he didn't have it right then. I don't know what he owed the man and I didn't want to know. All I knew was that I wanted to get the hell out of Dodge. I tried a little psychology on the guy and told him that I was sure by tomorrow, Steve would be able to give him what he wanted. Somehow, I convinced the guy to leave and settle this matter another time. I really thought he would have killed the both of us if I hadn't kept my cool and handled the situation the way I did.

When it comes down to serious matters like this, I am able to keep my composure and manipulate the outcome to my favor. If only I'd had the confidence to know, I could have done this all along. I found this secret out later in life when I surrendered to the drama and began creating what I wanted rather than what I didn't want. Ah, yes, more life lessons.

With the freedom that came with not being in a relationship, I drifted from one man to another. This really wasn't my thing; however, I didn't care for anyone enough to stay with them for too long.

I traveled with a guy who was a manager for a group called Lightening Fire. We went to Paris and London. I just wanted to go along for the ride. While in Paris, I decided to leave him and the tour, since I didn't enjoy his company. I took the train to Munich to visit my Amo. She was still in great shape, and teased me that I had gained a few pounds. I wasn't heavy, but I was very muscular. She was what you would call a fashionista today, and my muscular body was not her idea of femininity. She liked model thin. I always felt comfortable around her though, so I didn't mind her criticism.

Over the next two years, I went through a few more men and another abortion. Like I always did when in need of quick money, I went back to serving. I was not happy with my choices, but I didn't know what else to do. I was too immature to take care of a baby. I felt awful about this. I was just sleepwalking through my life.

⁓⁓⁓

Waitressing was a way to earn cash instantly and be among people, which I enjoyed at times. I worked with this group of Irish students who came over from Dublin. One of them was a young man by the name of John. He had such a cute baby face that I was very attracted to. I wanted him, and I put my antennas up to make that perfectly clear. It wasn't long before we were a couple. He was a few years my junior but that didn't matter to either of us. I didn't love him; I just lusted for him. We enjoyed a summer of fun until it was time for him to go back to Ireland. That didn't fly with me, so what did I do? I followed him to Dublin. I just had to be with him.

He lived at home with his mom and two sisters. I don't remember if his father was deceased or his mom was divorced, but his father was not around. It was cold, damp, and gray there. Not my kind of weather. During the late '70s and early '80s, Ireland was very depressed. Young students came to the States to work since there was no work to be had there. I slept with a hot water bottle every night. The food was horrible—pigeon, really? The bars closed at 9:00 PM sharp. You could feel the depression in the air; it was on everybody's face. As much as I adored John, I had to leave Ireland. His mother was very nice and I was shocked that she actually allowed me into her home. A twenty-four-year-old woman with her young nineteen-year-old son wouldn't go over too well with many moms. I wasn't feeling too well because I was pregnant again. I was just a fertile little bunny.

I got restless and booked myself a flight to Munich again. My old stomping grounds, my safe haven when I needed to get away and regroup. I spent time with my great Uncle Oskar. He was such a calming influence in my life and a strong male role model for me. He never married nor had any children. After a few weeks there, I headed back home.

I decided to have another abortion. I felt so horrible about doing this over and over again. My hormones were all out of whack, and I was really depressed. I needed to find work because my money situation was tight, so I got a job at a night club. It was the hottest club around and I was a cocktail waitress. I hated it. I was treated as a sex object. A sex thing. It was owned and operated by the Mafia. I was sure most of the money that got this place started was from the Lufthansa heist that took place back in 1976. There was a lot of Mafia in this area of Long Island.

I never did like the nightlife. I was more of a homebody type, but I needed to earn money and this provided a salary. John and I wrote love letters back and forth. I did miss him. Or I missed the thought of being in love. I didn't love myself, so how could I love anyone else? Like most people, I continued to search for it outside of my self. I was looking for a way out of this despicable cocktail waitressing job, but wasn't sure how I was going to leave. I liked having money, so I stuck it out.

My subconscious mind was ready, willing, and able to find my next venture and I found it. It came in the form of a man. Wow, what a revelation! These patterns run deep—men, waitressing, losing homes, and abusing myself. He was an old friend from elementary and high school. Edward walked in to the night club, and I immediately knew he was my way out. I was so happy to see a familiar face. I knew right then and there that he was my next. Unfortunately, I had to write a "Dear John" letter to dear John, because I was now with another man.

Anyone's head would spin with all these men. I was always looking for my father's love, which I never got from him. It wasn't until I learned to give myself that unconditional love, that I would stop bouncing around, choosing relationships that were either abusive, codependent, or unhealthy in some way.

But Edward was a healthier influence in my life at the time. I decided to go back to school. I enrolled in college and took some liberal arts classes, science courses such as oceanography and biology, and psychology classes as well. I loved them all. Edward owned his own woodworking shop with two other partners—a woman, whom he'd lived with for a while, and another guy. He was fairly successful and earning decent money. He had a young daughter, Janelle, from a previous marriage. His first wife had been my best friend in kindergarten. Coincidence? Again, I don't think so; it was just the way things were manifesting at the time.

Catherine, his first wife, had Janelle when she was only eighteen. Wow, I could have had three children by now myself, I thought. I've always felt guilty about having those abortions, but that was my choice at the time. Ed and Catherine weren't married very long. Edward told me he really hadn't wanted a child or to get married, but thought it was the right thing to do at the time. Obviously it didn't last. I loved the fact that he had a little girl that I could nurture when she was over at his apartment. I moved into his place within the year. I moved fast in relationships. Too fast. I was very spontaneous and never thought things through. Janelle gave me the stability I needed to think of someone else. I was ready for a child now. I was having fun with her. She was only four when I met her and we became pals quickly. It relieved Edward from the pressure of having to entertain her as well.

When I received my associates' degree, I decided to do something other than waitressing. Ah, breaking the pattern—shattering. I got a job at a florist's shop. I was employed by three gay partners. It was here that I got the confidence to eventually branch out on my own. They gave me their maintenance accounts. I would go to people's homes or businesses and take care of their live plants. Since I always had a green thumb and had gone to night school for horticulture when I lived upstate with Frank, this was a breeze for me. I was on my own, meeting people from different places, and developing my own style.

Edward and I wanted a larger place, so we moved from his one-bedroom apartment to a small house. It was a charming little home with a front porch. We had a yard to plant some vegetables and I was in heaven. I'd always wanted a family and a nice home. At least that was the illusion in my mind of what I thought I wanted. What I really wanted was to love myself enough that wherever I was and whomever I was with, I was comfortable in my own skin and could stop searching outside of myself for these things.

We were happy in these days. I wasn't drinking or doing drugs. I had a day job and was home in the evenings. Life was good. After a year of working for the florists, I had the idea of branching out on my own and starting a horticultural business. I figured if these guys could do it, so could I. I wasn't sure how on earth they were able to even run a business. Their lifestyle was so out of control. Sometimes I would come to work in the morning and find them sleeping on the floor, hungover from being out all night. They looked much older than they actually were, due to their life style. My life looked like a walk in the park compared to the things they were doing.

I got my DBA (doing business as) certificate and for the first time owned a business. It was awesome. Now I had to get clients. I went out to companies and shops with a business card and lots of personality. It worked! Little by little I was building a reputation for myself and earning a good income. I continued my education and was always learning new things about plants and soil. After a while I incorporated the business and named it Pleasing Plants, Inc. I was a professional, and I was good at what I did. It was a one-woman operation. I did it all. I was now twenty-eight and ready for that child. I conceived without a problem. This time I would go full term. I worked throughout my pregnancy with little discomfort, but I blew up like a helium balloon. I had to have a sense of humor since I didn't know what was bigger—my belly, my breasts, or my butt. I gained seventy pounds and loved every ounce! I fully enjoyed being pregnant. I had never felt better, physically or mentally. I didn't feel this way when I got pregnant before. I was always depressed and nauseous almost from the beginning prior to this pregnancy. But now, I was so ready for a child.

# CHAPTER 14

E dward and I decided to get married when I was about four months pregnant. We went off to Martha's Vineyard. There, we had a Justice of the Peace marry us on the beach; it was a humble, and quiet service.

We moved to a bigger place. It was a three-bedroom apartment with an open concept living, dining, and kitchen area with a pool in the back yard. I was able to walk into town, which I loved, and my commute to the homes and businesses I maintained was not a far drive. Everything seemed to be easy, breezy, and smooth. We had two cats, Spike and Felimina, who were brother and sister. I love animals. Life was good.

On January 21 at 11:22 PM, my darling little Naomi was born. Naomi Devonian. She was eight pounds, nine ounces. I had a natural delivery without any medications.

I was totally and completely in love with this little girl. Her smell, her skin, her soul was so delicious. Naomi was such a miracle to me. I took her home the next day. No long hospital stays for me. Unfortunately, Edward's mother's husband passed away on the same day Naomi was born. There was birth and death on the same day; the ebb and flow of life. I was too happy to be sad. I was glad he was out of pain, since he had been very sick the last few years of his life.

I hired someone to take over my business for a few weeks until I was feeling strong enough to go back to work. I decided to nurse Naomi, which was very natural for me. She was a restless sleeper and very hungry. Every two to three hours she was up nursing. I would nurse her on the couch and fall asleep with her on my chest. I never minded it. I just loved to smell her head. I was intoxicated by it.

When Naomi was about three months old, I took the cats to get shots for feline leukemia. I remember driving home, bringing the cats into the house and going back out shopping with Naomi in the car seat. After a few hours of being away, we came home and I found Spike dead under the dining room table. I was mortified. He'd had an allergic reaction to the shot. It happens to one out of every ten thousand cats. Spike was the one. He was such a good cat. Felimina wound up getting hit by a car when she was very young and developed seizures. I had her on phenobarbital, which kept the seizures at bay, but she always was in a zombie-like state. One day, she got out of the house and was away too long. Since she needed the medication every few hours, she probably had a seizure, got lost, and never returned home. That was the end of having pets for a while.

After losing her husband, Edward's mother, Pat, moved in with us. She didn't have much money, and didn't drive, so we thought it was best that she be with us. Pat was a simple woman and very good with children. It gave me the opportunity to go back to work without having a stranger watch my baby. I felt really good about that. She was easy-going and I got along with her really well. I nursed Naomi for about five months until I went back to work. She was still waking up every few hours and I would get up with her at night. She was a demanding little one.

All the weight I'd put on during my pregnancy was starting to dwindle away. But I was so determined to lose it that I got too thin. I went from 185 pounds, which was huge for me, to 98 pounds. I looked emaciated. I have a strong will and determination when I put my mind to something. I didn't like being that thin, so I was able to get back up to 113 pounds, which was an ideal weight for my height and frame.

My mom came over often to see little Naomi. She loved having a grandchild. My mom had a boyfriend for a while, but it was never an intimate kind of relationship. She'd met him at the coat factory she worked in for a few years. He called her Dr. Mathews; why, I don't know. Maybe because she was always eating natural, healthy foods. She called him Mr. Weiss. They never addressed each other by their first names. This was very odd to me, but hey, they liked each other. Unfortunately, he developed brain cancer and eventually passed away from it. My mom, who had been just fifty when he died, never started another romantic relationship. Naomi became her focus of attention. Actually, between the two grandmothers, Naomi was doted over like she was the last princess. She had them wrapped around her little pinky. Maybe we should have named her Lola.

Edward's business was expanding and doing well. My business was steady and I was earning good money, too. I loved working with plants and I was developing a good reputation. Edward was always designing homes in his spare time. He came across an ad in the paper about some homes that were going to be built. They were tearing down Guy Lombardo's house in Freeport and were going to build five new homes on the property. Edward was intrigued and saw an opportunity to build his design on one of the plots. We called and inquired about it. The next thing you know we were building our dream home. Out of the five houses that were being built, ours was the only one that was different. The two on the left and the two on the right of our house were standard builders' models. We were to have Guy's boat slip, too.

Building a home from the ground up is something that takes time. They said it would be about a year before we could move in. We were in no rush, so that was fine. I was busy raising little Naomi, juggling a relationship with my husband, a business, dealing with design elements for the new home, and taking care of an existing home. It was all good, though. I could do it all. That's what I thought. That's what I always thought. The house was being built to the specification of Edward's plan and design. We thought we could move in by the end of the year, which was drawing closer. I told our landlord that we would not be renewing the lease since we were going to be moving to our new home. Unfortunately, homes take a lot longer to build than anticipated. The landlord rented our place to someone else, so there was no turning back. We needed to look for temporary residence. Edward was pretty furious about this. He thought I should have negotiated something with the landlord. His temper was beginning to emerge more and more. We looked in the paper every day for places to live and there were places that were renting monthly or by the season, in The Hamptons. We found a great winter rental there. These places are fully furnished so we didn't need to unpack our stuff other than our personal belongings. We had put our furniture in storage to make things easy when it came time to move again into our new home. My commute to work, needless to say, was much longer. Somehow I didn't mind it. It gave me time to think and unwind. The Hamptons were beautiful in the winter. It was very quiet, not like it is in the summer months when things are hopping. I preferred this, as I enjoy being away from the crowds.

The winter came and went and the house still wasn't ready, so we had to move again. We found another place, about twenty minutes away. It was a beautiful older home in a very exclusive area. There were deer everywhere. It was kind of fun moving around checking out these different places, but on the other hand I wanted to be settled. We stayed here for a couple of months before finally moving into our new home in the summer of 1987.

When our new home was finished, it was gorgeous. It had a wall of glass overlooking the canal in the back, where fishing boats would cruise in and out of the harbor. Across the canal was the Nautical Mile. There were restaurants all along this street, one after another. It was a big party scene in the summer. Pat had her own mini-apartment on the upper level. Edward built in a small kitchenette for her so that she could have her own space and we could have our privacy.

Things were getting busier and busier. Edwards's business was growing even bigger and he hired a new draftsman by the name of Paul. I was busy with designing and installing plants for a huge Mercedes, BMW, and Rolls Royce dealership. They had just completed building a multimillion dollar car showroom and wanted a sixteen-foot planter in the center of it where the salesman would sit around.

It seemed like time was speeding up. By September of 1987, I was pregnant again. Everyone was happy and our family was growing. My due date was May 21, 1988, which also happened to be Edward's birthday. It seemed like there were a lot of 21's in my life. Naomi was born on January 21st. My father was born on March 21st and passed on April 21st. When I have something fixed in my mind, I just know it will manifest that way. Lilly was born on her due date. She was seven pounds, ten ounces. She looked so much like Naomi, but was a bit smaller. She was also much more serene. Lilly slept through the night after only three weeks. The pregnancy went smoothly and again, I took no medication. They both were easy labors. I was very blessed.

# CHAPTER 15

Now that I had two children, a husband, a mother-in-law, my business, Edward's business, my mom coming over all the time, and Edward's older daughter Janelle coming every other weekend, I was feeling overwhelmed. I didn't have the skills I do now to calm down and meditate. Our home was a busy place and our backyard seemed like party central. We didn't even have window treatments to shut off the sights that were passing by continuously on the waters. I wasn't sure if this was the place I wanted to raise the girls. I really liked living in Litchfield, where life was slower and more peaceful. Since Edward loved it out there, too, and had a thing for moving, he agreed to sell the house and look for a rental. The market was really good at the time and my intuition told me that we would sell the house for our asking price and I was right on the money. We made a good profit and were on to our next home.

Since we had loved it so much, we decided to go back to the Hamptons. We found a relatively large house to suit our needs. Little did I know, we would be taking on an unwanted roommate. Paul, the guy who Edward hired as a draftsman, was becoming a new member of our family. I think this was the beginning of the end of our marriage. Although I liked Paul, I didn't want him living with us, especially since Edward gave him the master suite, which was a huge bedroom with an en suite bathroom. I guess he thought it would be like an apartment in the house for him; however, I felt it was an intrusion on our privacy. Not only did he have Paul living with us, he converted the dining room into his in-home office. Edward was so headstrong that I didn't have a say in the matter. I am headstrong too, and though we would often buck heads, he usually won.

So, now we had Edward's mother, Paul, and Edward's business, all under one roof. I am willing to sacrifice things for the greater good, but I just couldn't see the vision here. Often, Edward would go out for power lunches with Paul that entailed alcohol. He would come back to the dining room/office to work. Paul, who was slow as molasses, wouldn't have some drawing ready for him, so I would hear these blood-curdling screams coming out of Edward's mouth, berating Paul for not performing. It was sheer hell.

Lilly was only a year old and Naomi three. They were the cutest little girls; I absolutely adored them. I signed Naomi up for pre-kindergartn. There were many celebrities whose children attended this school. We would see them all at school fundraisers and events. Summers in the Hamptons were wonderful. We had a big pool in the back yard, which we took full advantage of. The kids loved swimming with their floaties.

At this time, Edward was changing his business around, doing things that I was not aware of. He had separated with the partners he had and changed the name of his business. One day while he was out on one of his power lunches and I was home with the kids, the phone rang. I answered it and someone on the line from the business bureau, or at least that is what they said. They were inquiring about Edward's business. They asked a few questions, which I naively and innocently answered. I mentioned this to Edward as he returned home, thinking nothing of it. Well, he showed me some of his wrath like I had never seen before. It was if my father had been reborn and I was getting walloped. I was humiliated, shamed, shocked, and distraught. I ran out of the house, hysterical, and just kept on running. I couldn't believe he would ever scream at me like that. I stayed away for hours, until sunset. Thank God, his mother was there to watch the kids. I knew from that moment on that I would spiritually, mentally, and physically separate myself from him. It was over.

I went through the motions of being with him and we stayed together for a number of years afterward, but I never had sex with him again. I didn't even think he minded. He was so involved with his business that he became a workaholic. Edward had started smoking pot while he was designing our Guy Lombardo house. I didn't think much of it then and joined him on occasion. But now he was smoking it a lot, and had been drinking more, too. He was a functioning alcoholic, if there even is such I thing. He was only functioning in the sense that he was able to do his job. His life was falling apart at the seams, but he didn't see it.

My life was unraveling, too. I was looking for my way out again. My subconscious mind was busy at work searching for the right opportunity to sabotage the marriage and find my escape hatch. I was looking for a new plan.

I didn't rush anything. The girls were young and I really didn't want to disrupt their lives. I had to think of what was best for them, too. In the meantime, I took the girls to Europe a few times, visiting family in Munich. Edward never wanted to go, so I went with my mom or by myself. If Edward would have shown the slightest bit of remorse or tried to make amends in some way, I might have had the desire to work things out with him; but he never did. Sadly, we were drifting apart. Although we were separated in spirit, we still shared the same bed and moved forward in planning our lives together.

We'd made a good amount of money on the sale of our home and Edward was looking to purchase something else. He found a big old Stanford home, just East of where we had been. It was in need of major updating, and Edward saw it as an opportunity to renovate and sink his energy into. I was looking at the landscape aspect of the home. It had mature trees, shrubs, and plants.

Edward's idea was to gut the whole house and redo everything from floor to roof. It was a huge undertaking. I went along with him since I didn't argue with him too much anymore. My heart wasn't in the relationship, so I just agreed with things unless they pertained to the children, me, or my business. We wound up buying the house and beginning renovations.

Our lease was up on the house we were renting so we moved into a rental closer by to supervise the renovations. This was a magnificent, old country-like home. It was semi-neglected but livable, with a huge backyard leading to a lake and our own private beach. The kitchen was old, with a cast iron oven. It had a living room with a massive stone fireplace. The house was falling apart but it was funky and fun to live in for a short time. We had a grape orchard next to the three-car garage, and a long driveway that circled around the front yard. The garage must have at one time held horses because there was a hay chute in it.

There was a happy vibe about the house. We always had a lot of company and parties here. Even though Edward and I were not in a harmonious sync, we managed to fake it to the outside world. Inside, I thought I was yearning for the love of a man, but I was really seeking myself. I met a man at City Motors while I was maintaining the plants there. Phillip was a car wholesaler who had just bought a new apartment in Manhattan. He was looking for a designer to alter the layout and design of it, since it was older and needed work. We became friendly and I mentioned that my husband was an architectural woodworker and designer.

Phillip gave me his contact number, which I gave to Edward. The two of them hit it off and developed a friendship and business relationship.

Edward got the contract and began working on Phillip's apartment, which was on the twenty-third floor of a building on the upper west side. Phillip also hired me to do the landscaping on his outdoor terrace.

Phillip was best friends with one of the owners of City Motors; a gentleman by the name of Tom Kartian, who also lived in New York. He wanted me to take a look at his apartment so that I could offer him my horticultural advice. He was very rich and extremely charismatic; he had a way of charming people to do what he wanted.

Tom Kartian was a self-made multi-millionaire. His father was from Armenia and his mother was from Paris, where he was born. He was an only child and came over to the United States when he was just a young boy. His father died before they came over. His mother did not have much money to support them and took on a maid position to get by. They lived very humbly. When he was nineteen, his mother died. Here you have a young man, with both parents deceased and no siblings, finding his way in the Big Apple. The fortitude and determination that some people have amazes me. Their will to survive and thrive is strong. Is it luck? Timing? Destiny? Or is it a combination of all these things? Is it a dream? A plan? A desire? Or is it God's will? I am fascinated by these rags-to-riches stories. I love to uncover what it is that made these people who they are.

I agreed to meet Tom at his place. It was early evening when I arrived at the building, which is loaded with history. Many celebrities were living there and still do. The first time I entered Tom's second-floor apartment, I felt like I'd just walked into a museum. It was a masterpiece. His taste was impeccable. He knew exactly what he wanted and got it. The dark, detailed woodwork, high ceilings, and gargoyles engraved in the fireplaces; these were just a few of the features that stood out to impress anybody that walked by. Everything was in order and perfect, from the custom draperies on the windows to the original oriental carpets on the floor. The dining room walls and ceiling were hand-stenciled. He had paintings from well-known artists that I learned he sometimes loaned to museums for exhibits. There must have been at least two million dollars' worth of furniture in his living room alone. I was in awe.

After he gave me a tour of his place, Tom showed me where he wanted to put the live kentia palms. Those were the only plants he wanted; he felt they would fit in well with his decor. Like everything else in the apartment, they were one of the most expensive plants money could buy.

He offered me a glass of wine, which I did not refuse. Little did I know, he had plans to seduce me that evening. Well, if the truth be told, I knew what he was up to; I just played dumb. Eureka! I had found my way out of the relationship with Edward. Or at least this was the beginning of the way out. Did I subconsciously set this all up, since I was looking for an escape? Of course I did. If I were truly in love with Edward, I would never have allowed this to take place. I knew I'd put on a flirtatious act and Tom had picked up on it.

An affair blossomed and I had a new focus. Tom would leave me the keys to his place so that I could come whenever I wanted. I would arrive early and wait for him to come home. It was a total fantasy for me. I was becoming obsessive. How Edward didn't know something was up is beyond me, but I hid this relationship well.

The house that we were renovating in the Hamptons was taking shape. It was gutted and reframed from the inside, had all new windows installed, and a new roof placed. From the outside looking in, my life appeared to be perfect; but in reality, it was falling apart. I was building a house of cards and it was only a matter of time before it would all come crumbling down. There was no love between Edward and I; and where there is no love, there is no hope for the future. But we managed to play this game for a while longer.

# CHAPTER 16

I
t was now the summer of 1991. Lilly had finished nursery school and Naomi had graduated from the first grade.

Pat was still living with us and so was Paul. Everyone was beginning to feel the pressure of our relationship coming to a boiling point. Edward would scream at his mom for reasons that were irrational, and continued to rage at Paul if he didn't complete his work. Paul was like a teenage son I'd never asked for. We bailed him out of a DWI and other escapades. Paul had what I called the mañana syndrome: "Why do today what you can put off until tomorrow?" My brother, who was around frequently, said that Paul had three speeds: slow, slower, and stop. He was talented, just not very productive.

Around this time, Edward said he wanted to take over the books from my business. I think he was strapped for cash and wanted to control my books so that he'd have access to the money. I was making a good income; I contributed to the household, bought the groceries, and took care of the children's needs. There was no way I was relinquishing control of my business. I was organized and used QuickBooks, so it wasn't like there were issues with my bookkeeping. He just wanted control, and I wasn't going to give it to him.

I ended my relationship with Tom Kartian because I saw that I was not the only woman he was seducing. I would often come to his apartment to maintain the plants in the morning and find a woman just leaving. I wanted to keep a business relationship with him, so I never allowed my emotions to jeopardize our connection.

We'd never actually had intercourse. He wasn't capable of being that intimate. He had weird sexual fetishes that needed to be fulfilled; for instance, he really enjoyed phone sex. I obliged to keep the connection alive, but I wasn't enjoying being a part of it anymore. It was only causing me confusion when I wanted to find some peace.

I was looking in all the wrong places to find that peace. I never bothered to look within. I wasn't aware that peace of mind comes through discipline and quieting of the mind. My mind then was like a huge ball of twisted wire.

---

Edward's business was taking a big hit from what was called "Black Monday." In 1987, the stock market had taken a big plunge; however, it took a few years for the effects to trickle down to Edward's line of work. If we were both on the same page and had a strong vision, I don't believe this would have affected us as it did. We were over-extended with renovating a house, paying rent, and running his business. He kept on taking out cash advances, so now we were incurring debt. I suggested that we buy or rent an inexpensive motor home and live on the property of the new home, but he didn't want anything to do with that. He liked living large and didn't want to stop now. I liked it, too, but I saw we were heading for financial trouble and I was willing to make sacrifices for the good of our future well-being. Edward and I fought all the time, so I was always looking to escape being around him. One day, while I was working in the city on Phillip's terrace, Phillip seduced me. We had sex, and I regretted it afterward. It seemed like all men just wanted to have sex with me. There was more to me than just a body. I knew I had an amazing body and good looks, and I knew that I radiated sensuality; however, there was something more about me that was attracting these men to me. I was too weak to say no and stand my ground. This was still my pattern—trying to fill the void and find the love of my father. Men were an addiction for me and I needed them to love me. But it didn't work. I was only left empty and lonely.

This time Edward knew something was up. I was gone way too long and he asked me where I had been. We were in our bedroom on the opposite side of the children's' room and his Mom's quarters. I didn't want to lie anymore, so I told him the truth about everything. I told him that Phillip and I had had sex, and I told him about my affair with Tom. I wanted to clear my conscience. It felt good to finally be up-front and not hide any more.

Edward was furious. He beat me to a pulp. He broke a few ribs, gave me several black-and-blue marks, and banged my head so hard I even had bruises on my face. I did not fight back; I took it all. I rationalized that I deserved it; that it was my punishment. It was one of my lowest points in my life. His mother, Paul, and the kids didn't know what had happened. We were in our bedroom late at night, and the next day I made up some lie about how I'd gotten my bruises. From then on, I knew that it was over.

Often he did not come home at night and I didn't ask any questions. The wounds that were inflicted on me slowly healed, but the internal ones stayed open. That hurt remains until you learn to heal from the inside out. It would be a while before I learned how to do this.

Before this violent episode occurred, Edward had convinced the landlord to fix up a few things and paint areas of the house, since it was neglected and needed the work. The landlord agreed to this, as long as Edward hired the labor and oversaw the work himself. He hired a man by the name of Cooper. Where he found him I have no idea. He wasn't licensed or insured. Cooper was a rugged Marlboro man. He drove an old, blue Chevy and was very good-looking. I was attracted to him immediately. When I was home, I would see him work and we would engage in conversation.

After my emotional break from Edward, Cooper and I got closer and closer. He was a drinker, smoker, and partier. I was in such a vulnerable place in my life that I began smoking and drinking with him. I'd done it on and off before then, but now it was full on. We would go out often to parties and socialize with people who were also drinking and drugging. I wanted to belong, so I went with it. I often drank way too much and got sick. I was a happy-go-lucky drunk. Everything was great; I was over-generous and gave everything away, including myself. The next day, I would be hugging the toilet. As much as I hated myself for this, I continued on this rampage for quite a while.

Edward found himself a young lady friend who was filling his needs, too. We were both acting like stupid, immature teenagers. We were foreclosing on the house we'd bought and owed the banks more money than I could have imagined. I was looking to move out of the house we were renting since it was too big. I wanted to start over. Edward's mother Pat moved to a small apartment close by to get away from all the chaos that was taking place. The girls would either go over there or I would pick her up when I needed her to babysit. Paul moved out too—amazing!

Cooper told me about a house in the neighborhood that he was painting for a real estate agent. It was a small hamlet on the East end of the island. I went to see the house. It was a small

Cape Cod with about a half-acre of land. The kitchen was old but clean, the living room had a brick fireplace and a large bay window. I knew right away that I wanted this house. I knew the real estate broker who was renting the house, so I called and told him I wanted it. He said that it was already in negotiations to be rented to someone else. I needed that house and wanted him to do whatever it took to squash that deal and make it mine. He did, and it was.

It was the perfect place to begin yet again. I thought I had the strength, determination, and willpower to raise the girls on my own. But my needs kicked in again, and I rushed to fill them as usual. I asked Cooper to move in. He agreed. Why wouldn't he? I was hardworking, a good cook, good looking, and good in bed. What's not to like? My darling little Naomi wasn't too happy about this. Lilly didn't seem to mind so much. Naomi needed my attention and she didn't want to share me with him. I don't blame her. It was a time in my girls' lives where they needed me and I wasn't fully present. I was torn between them and Cooper. Cooper was very immature. He came from an Irish-Catholic background and the school of hard knocks, so there wasn't anything soft and cuddly here. He liked to drink, and drink some more. I liked my pot. We both liked having sex. Since my hormones were still coursing through me, I was always ready.

I was happy here, or at least there was the illusion of being happy. I had a man, my children, a home, a business, and a garden. What more could I ask for? I was also going through a divorce and bankruptcy at the same time. Thank God for my business, since all the money Edward and I had together was untouchable. The IRS froze our bank accounts. He had somehow neglected to pay his taxes, which resulted in a lien. I had to keep my accounts totally separate. Since we both didn't have much, we agreed on an amicable settlement. All I wanted was $500.00

a month for child support; nothing else. He agreed and we both were free of our marriage.

We got along so much better once we were separated. We did buck heads once in a while when we had a disagreement about the girls, but for the most part we were able to remain friends. He never was that involved as a father so anything I did was usually alright with him. I had always wanted him to play a more active role with the girls; but he just didn't. He'd never even changed a diaper when the girls were babies. I know he loved the girls but he just couldn't fully engage in playing the role of dad. I think he enjoyed being a weekend dad more.

———— ∿∾∘∾⟳⟲∾∘∾∿ ————

Because of my bankruptcy, my credit was shot for seven years. I was diligent and determined to regain it. Living with Cooper was a codependent relationship. He needed me to keep things together and I needed him for a false sense of love. It was like walking on egg shells when he was drunk though. Sometimes he got nasty and mean. Other times he was happy-go-lucky. It all depended on the mood he was in before he started drinking.

The name of our new street was Rabbit Road. How perfect— because not long after we moved in, this fertile bunny got pregnant again. I was just beginning to feel like I had some wiggle room to explore more of life, and now there was a little one wiggling inside of me. The last thing I wanted was another child. So I had another abortion. Since money was so tight, and Cooper didn't have any, I pawned some jewelry to pay for it. I had a beautiful cocktail ring that my father had brought me from China, along with a synthetic ruby with real diamonds around it from my grandmother Betty, I sold them both. All went well and I was back on my feet within a day. My hormones were out of control again. I was depressed one minute, angry the next, and not sure what was going to come up as the days went by. I needed to get myself stabilized. I finally went on birth control for a few years after this, since I didn't want to ever go through this again.

The girls were adjusting to our new home. Children are resilient, but I know they wanted some stability. Edward rented a large home about a mile and half away, which was good for the girls since they knew he was fairly close by. Regardless, divorce affects children. They are very sensitive and intuitive, and they know when something isn't right. They need to be reassured that they aren't the cause of their parents' bad behavior. What we don't fix, our children inherit. We just pass the dysfunction down from one generation to the next, until we become aware of the problem and do something to change it.

———— ∿∿⦿⦿⦿∿∿ ————

There was a two-room schoolhouse in our town that Naomi and Lilly attended. Lilly started Kindergarten there and Naomi was going into her fourth year. To get to school, all you had to do was cut through our backyard, cross the street and you were there. About twenty-three children altogether attended the school, from kindergarten to sixth grade. Some years there were less. It was known as The Little Red Schoolhouse. I believe there were only two schools like this remaining in the state.

It had its pros and cons, like any other school. Across the street from our home was a family with three children, Glenda, who was a year younger than Naomi; Rob, who was a year older; and Sara, who was already a teenager. I thought that raising children here would be a wonderful experience, with little influence from all the riffraff of a larger town. I couldn't have been more wrong. When I first met little Glenda, it was after school and all the girls had come over to my house. The first thing I heard out of Glenda's mouth was, "Let's put our shit down here." I thought I was hearing things; she was only in first grade! Are you kidding? Who were these kids? I was outraged. I asked her to not talk like that in my home. She just looked at me with this glazed-out stare. On the first day of school, I took a picture of all the girls outside on the neighbor's fence. I didn't notice it at the time but when I looked at the picture after I took it, Glenda had her middle finger up. I decided to go over her house and meet the parents. They were as loose as their kids were. The stepfather ran a rehab center; though I think he had a major drug problem himself. The mother was very timid and unresponsive. They had raised their kids with foul mouths and no respect. I knew I wasn't any angel; however, I would not condone my children cursing or having poor manners like that. Well, these were the kids on the block. There was another family on the corner lot who were hoarders. Their house was literally falling apart and they had blue tarps over everything. No outsider was ever invited into their house, either. The two girls, Pat and Roberta, had a horrific odor about them. If you looked through the windows you could see junk piled up to the windowsills. Welcome to life on Rabbit Road.

There was one other family who lived directly across from us, the Manganas. They were an elderly Italian couple, Maryanne and Jerry. Jerry was as prejudiced as the day is long. Any time I would go over to say hello, he would talk about the Jews and how Hitler should have killed them all. Ignorance and fear—that is what prejudice is all about. Somehow, I never took offense. I saw right through him and knew that he was all talk. Maryanne would wonder why I was living here with Cooper. She saw something in me that was more than just a country bumpkin. She always encouraged me to broaden my horizons. Not that Cooper was a bad guy; he was who he was, but that's all he was. I was always looking to grow, expand, learn, and meet new people. I think Maryanne saw this and knew Cooper was comfortable where he was. Though I wanted more, I was enmeshed in the relationship now and I wanted to make it work.

Cooper did like to travel and he came to Europe with me and the girls on several occasions. Of course we went to Munich during Oktoberfest. He got piss drunk, as so many people did. I, too, had more than I should have. But my family there really liked him. He could be very charming, quick-witted, and friendly when he wanted to. He also could be jealous, cold, sharp-tongued, and angry. I didn't know when he would be the friendly, nice Cooper or the mean, cold Cooper. When we fought, I would retreat and become quiet, while he wanted to talk. I think in most relationships the opposite is true: women are the ones who want to talk things out and the men retreat. But I was like the man in the relationship. I was the one who had a business and brought in the majority of the income; I handled the bills and all the responsibilities. He was like a teenager wanting to have a good time. When we went out together, he had to make sure that I wasn't talking or paying attention to any other man. He would become extremely jealous and interrogate me if he had suspected something.

Cooper sometimes worked for me and often came with me to do landscaping jobs. Again, if I were to talk to anyone that he thought was a threat, I would hear about it. He wanted all my attention, all of the time. The days I went to work without him and I was late coming home, he would be fuming when I returned. It was awful to live like this, but that is what I managed to do for about seven years. Then, I think I got the seven-year itch.

We couldn't have been more different. He had a large family; I had a very small family. He was Irish-Catholic; I was German-Jewish. My family believed in education; his believed in ... I am not sure what. He had three brothers. His older brother, Jesse, was mentally unstable, lived in and out of group homes, and took medication daily. Sometimes he had to be committed to a psychiatric ward if something triggered him. His two younger brothers, Garret and Cassidy, were tough and wild guys who got into a lot of trouble. When they were teenagers, they'd robbed a jewelry store, assaulted the owner, and fled the scene of the crime. The police tracked them down since they had a record of breaking into houses in their neighborhood. Cassidy got five years in prison since he was the one who had the weapon; Garrett got probation. They reminded me of the McCoys from the old west. Even their names were from some old western: Cooper, Garret, Jesse, and Cassidy Calhoun. I think they had an overload of testosterone that made them so wild. Cooper also had two sisters, Celeste and Laura. All the Calhouns were very attractive. The girls were beautiful and the guys very handsome. The mom raised the girls to find good providers, which they did. But the boys were raised to find good providers, too, and I know Cooper found one.

Cassidy found God in jail and became a born-again Christian, which transformed his life. He'd also had an opportunity to study and become a doctor while in prison. He was very bright and he succeeded. His payback was that when he got out, he had to do pro bono work for a number of years until his education was repaid. In addition to that, he got married while in prison and soon had a clan of his own.

I wish Cooper could have been transformed like that. I think what Cooper and I had in common was the dysfunction that was handed down to us by our parents. His was different, but just as crazy. If he had been ready to change, or had somehow shown some sign of wanting to open up to healthier way of living, maybe things could have worked out between us, but he was perfectly happy with the status quo.

# CHAPTER 17

Something was starting to shift in me. I was beginning to change. I was going to the library and taking out audio books about personal development to listen to on my two-hour commute each way to and from my jobs. They started to open my mind to spiritual growth. I was getting restless living this stagnant life; I wanted more.

Glenda had moved and new neighbors moved into the house where she'd lived: a woman named Christina and her three kids, two teenage girls and a boy. At first I thought this was great. I would have babysitters for my girls. April and Liz, the two girls, seemed like perfect young ladies to hire and watch Naomi and Lilly when I needed to go out. How someone looks or seems from the outside can be very deceiving. The vibes of that house attracted some funky energy, in this case, drug energy. Christina's husband, Buddy, was in prison with a life sentence for drug trafficking. They owned a beautiful home on the water in New Jersey. There he would smuggle large quantities of marijuana onto shore. He owned some supermarkets that the money was laundered through. From what I heard, the authorities knew about the drug trade, but left him alone because he donated large amounts of money back into the community. Anything and everything was at their disposal. She could take a helicopter and fly into Manhattan to get her hair done; there were fancy cars, boats, and parties galore. Buddy's operation got bigger and they moved to a new town. Here, the people of the community did not cotton to new, flashy money. The girls were in private school and Jay, the boy, was just a baby when the feds raided their home. They arrested Buddy and confiscated everything. The party was over. Under the Rockefeller laws, they wanted to set an example and gave Buddy a life sentence. Christina would have to find her way alone with the kids. His family had sheltered a good part of his money, so Christina had a cushion to start over with. She went to school for cosmetology and started her life over. Christina seemed inflicted with the same handicap that I had: men! Men saw her money and her good looks and took advantage of her. She too was looking for love in all the wrong places and with all the wrong men. I have found this to be a common infliction with woman. A therapist I went to see while I was with Cooper recommended a book: *Women Who Love Too Much*. Yes, that described me, Christina, and many other women I came to know. The things we women do for love. If and when we discover our own power, we are a force that has the potential to change the world for good. I was beginning to do this, but for every step forward, I would take two steps back.

———

For a small, quiet town there was certainly a lot of drama. I became close friends with Christina. It is an interesting phenomenon how people become attracted to one another. The friends I choose and attracted were always interesting and led exciting lives.

Her two daughters had led privileged lives that came to an abrupt end. They had been yanked out of private school and into the public school system. I'm sure it must have been devastating for the whole family to go from riches to middle class.

I had discovered that the girls became addicted to heroin. I was shocked to find this out, especially because I had them babysit my girls on occasion. I didn't understand addiction to its full extent then, and I wouldn't until my own life was personally affected by its ravishing effects. Christina was a beautiful woman with an addiction and codependent tendency herself. She would continually bail her children out of situations, give them money, and enable them. They had gotten used to living an extravagant life that was no longer there. I guess they just wanted to escape the trappings of what they thought was a humdrum existence. They weren't prepared to deal with the world without the shelter and protection of their father and what his money could buy. Going from rags to riches is rewarding and gratifying, especially if you earned your way up. Then, you can handle a setback if it ever happens. But having everything you want, and then losing it all, is much harder.

There was no value system in place. Their money came from illegitimate means. They were playing a high-risk game where the stakes were volatile. I'm sure the girls saw a lot of activity that children should never have been exposed to. The law of cause and effect is always at work. We reap what we sow, for every action, there is an equal and opposite reaction. I, myself, was learning these lessons over and over.

———— ᠕᠊ᢀ᠊ᡐᠷᠲᢀᡐᢀ᠊ᡐ᠊ᠥᡍᡍ ————

Cooper was not too fond of my new friendship with Christina, but he didn't like me having *any* friendship that took me away from him. This was my codependent relationship.

One time in early October, Cooper, the girls, and I traveled to Germany. We stayed with my relatives for a week, then rented a car and drove to Venice, Italy. What should have been a wonderful vacation turned out to be an emotional nightmare. I don't remember exactly what set Cooper off, but he got into one of his funky moods and stayed in it for the entire trip. It was awful. How could you ruin Italy?—take a lousy relationship, mix it with alcohol, two young girls, a dash of a moody man, and voila, you get a spoiled mix. I should have learned my lesson but I didn't. I knew Cooper was volatile. I knew he got cranky with children around, but I decided to take this trip anyway.

I wanted to give my girls the gift of travel that I had been so privileged to receive. I took them to Washington, D.C., with Cooper. That trip, also, was compromised by his foul mood. We went to Disneyworld and although it was fun, I felt so uncomfortable at his sister's home, where we were staying, and so did Naomi. One of his sister's sons teased Naomi continuously and I was so upset by this. Time and time again, I subjected my children and myself to the torture of a way of being that I thought I could get used to. I was still mentally ill!

———∿∿⦿⟋⊙⟍⦿⟍⦿⟋⊙⟍∿∿———

The last family trip we took together was to Paris and then Munich. Christina, her new boyfriend at the time, and both of their sons came, too. This was a recipe for disaster, as the men didn't really get along. We arrived in Paris and from the very get-go, there were problems. Naomi was acting up, and for good reason. We visited Versailles, the Louvre, the Eiffel Tower, and many other attractions. We all enjoyed that part of the trip; but in our down time, personalities clashed and egos got in the way of being at ease with one another. After a week in Paris, we rented two cars and drove to Munich to visit and stay with my relatives again. Christina, her boyfriend, and their sons stayed at a nearby hotel. Again, they enjoyed the sights of the city but the men couldn't put their differences aside to find a common ground.

Why couldn't we just all get along? It was so immature to have such turmoil for no apparent reason.

I have learned that to create peace between people, you must try to understand the other person, even if you do not agree with their philosophies and ways of being. Find something that is good and expand on that.

We were all glad to get home and get back to our little world, to surround ourselves with the things that made us feel comfortable and secure. I believe we all grew a bit through that experience, even though there was such friction.

Life begins outside of our comfort zone. It stretches us to be more. Unfortunately most people don't like being uncomfortable. They like staying in their routine and being close to those things that they are familiar with. In order to have more, you must reach for more. Bob Proctor, one of my coaching teachers, once said, "If you're not living on the edge, you're taking up way too much room." That's not an easy thing to do, but necessary for a life filled with all the good you desire.

I was internally still unhappy with myself, and the reflection in my material world would reveal this. Could I take responsibility for creating all the craziness that was showing up in my life? I do now, but I didn't back then. I was still asleep to my spiritual nature.

# CHAPTER 18

Things were disintegrating rapidly between Cooper and I. I wanted the relationship to work, but I was unhappy. I was very busy at work. City Motors was expanding its outdoor landscaping and I was in charge of the project. Cooper felt he could do the work, so I gave him the opportunity to prove himself. I needed to rent heavy equipment and day laborers. It was a big job. I oversaw the project, which Cooper didn't like. He didn't like me being the boss and in charge. It can get complicated to work and live with someone. I was paying him good money to do the job, and it was eventually completed.

At the same time, I was traveling into the city twice a week providing fresh potted flowers for office buildings. I would leave at about 4:00AM on Sunday morning so that my clients would have fresh flowers for Monday, I would then go back midweek to maintain them. Sometimes Cooper would go, but most of the time it fell on me. Cooper had a hard time getting up that early and he kept pushing it off. Since it was my business, I took everything very seriously and wanted everything done impeccably. I would get angry at him if he took shortcuts.

I loved to listen to the motivational tapes I got from the library in the car while I was driving. They inspired me to reach, grow, and be a better person. I wanted Cooper to listen to them, too, but he wanted no part of it. He was beginning to take on more responsibility and I believe it had to do with all the changes that I was going through. I began to see that I'd helped him grow from a boy to a functioning man. I helped him get a van, insurance for that van, a bank account, and other things grownups do. I was good at seeing the potential in men. I could super-size them, make them into a better version of themselves. This, however, was only a distraction for me to focus on someone else, rather than see my own shortcomings. It is so much easier to see the faults in others and correct them than to see the faults in yourself and correct those.

I realized that if I continued to stay in this relationship, I would never be able to fulfill all of my desires and passions. I had to be honest with Cooper and myself, so I sat down with him and told him that I wanted to end the relationship. It took every ounce of strength to do this because I didn't want to hurt him. I was always trying to wiggle my way out of situations—sabotaging, having my partner leave me first, anything but being direct and up front. I hated the confrontation. But I did it. Cooper was not happy. Not only was he furious, he demanded money from me. He wanted me to pay him for lost time, or spite, or whatever. He knew I had saved quite a bit of money and wanted a part of it. I gave him a few thousand dollars, which hurt more emotionally than financially. Though it wasn't the easiest thing I've ever done, it certainly wasn't as difficult as I had made it out to be in my mind. That was all it took; Cooper was gone.

I was alone with my girls. Naomi was a young teenager and was acting out. Could you blame her? I remember how confused I was at her age and I'm sure she was confused, too. I wasn't the greatest role model for her. How could I have been? I didn't know any better myself. I did hug my girls all the time and let them know how much I loved them. That was a huge difference from my parents. I'd never received this kind of reassurance. Once Naomi left the little red schoolhouse to travel for junior high, things really took a turn for the worse. The school was predominantly white and homogenized. She didn't feel like she fit in, and was attracted to her fellow outcasts. I saw the change in her and I didn't like it. She became very rebellious and nasty, so I pulled her out and put her into a private Catholic school. We weren't religious, but I needed to take action. This was the only school in the area that gave me hope for her to change.

She did not want to go, or wear a uniform and conform to a more regimented way of schooling. At first she was unhappy. Little by little she began to enjoy it. But Naomi was always headstrong and she quickly found friends that were just as troubled as the ones in public school. She attracted the "bad girls." I guess they were more fun. I wasn't aware of this at the time, but Catholic schoolgirls can be more rebellious than public school kids. She finished the school year with so-so grades, never having really applied herself.

————— ✦✦✦ —————

That summer, I decided to become a certified reflexologist. I was already engaged in an online course for a bachelor's degree in natural health through Clayton College. I was studying many natural modalities of healing and became fascinated with holistic medicine. The new course ran from May through October. Every weekend, while the girls were with their father, I would travel into Manhattan for classes. I was fascinated by natural health and was totally engrossed in my newfound passion.

During this time, I developed Hygiea, a natural and organic body spray. I was on a creative streak. For the first time in my life, I was devoting time and energy to myself instead of to a man. It felt so good, and I had so much energy.

I was just completing my certificate when a curve ball was approaching.

———⁓ᵂ∘ᴏ❀⧉❀ᴏ∘ᵂ⁓———

About this time, a gentleman moved in next door for the winter. The house was used as a weekend summer home, and the owners would rent it out for the winter to offset their mortgage. I met him outside at his car as he was moving in and I was walking my dog. He introduced himself to me and he seemed very nice. The timing could not have been worse. I really believe God was giving me a test. Another man—and right next door?

His name was Ivan and he seemed like a great guy. I should have known better. A wolf disguised in sheep's clothing. How appearances can be so deceiving. It was too soon, and he was not the right guy. But it was so easy; he was right there. This was trouble.

We became friends. Ivan would invite me over for drinks and dinner. He was working at a country club in town that had recently opened. I was working there, too. I'd gotten the contract to install and maintain the plants in the clubhouse and create the exterior planters. He had been transferred to the food and beverage department to oversee the kitchen. I was there once a week, so I would see him there, too. He wasn't particularly good looking and was overweight. He was not my type—not that I had a type in mind. That was part of my dilemma; I needed to be specific if I wanted to attract the right man for me. I left it wide open to anyone. Anyway, the winter was approaching, and everything was slowing down. Ivan was like my new best friend. I should have seen the red flags; they were all around. My intuition was screaming at me. It was like Jiminy Cricket from Pinocchio was standing on my shoulders saying, "Don't do it; don't get into a relationship with him!" But I didn't listen. I wanted a man in my life, and he was my new subject. I had a project. I could get him healthy, help him lose weight, stop smoking, and get into shape. I saw the potential. Again, another distraction. So what did I do? I slept with him.

The sex wasn't even that good. But the minute I do this with a new man, I feel like some kind of attachment happens. Like I am bonded now and I have to stay with him. It is so strange how this feeling overcomes me. After that, Ivan was professing his love to me, way too early in the relationship. And I was falling for it; hook, line, and sinker. I was so desperate to be loved that I settled for the first guy who came along, the path of least resistance. Not a wise choice. Out of the blue, two months later, Ivan told me he was bored and wanted to move back to New Jersey. He wanted to continue our relationship, though, so we made plans to see each other every other weekend. Either he would come down to me or I would go up to him. Being the one who always put more effort in, I did most of the traveling. The weekends that Naomi and Lilly were at their dad's, I would take the three to four hour drive. Every time I went to see him, the warning signs were right in front of me. But I was in too deep now. He told me he wanted to marry me. He told me that we could have such a great life together. He told me so many false things that I was ripe for hearing. Things I'd never heard before. They sounded so good, but they were all lies. He was a sugar addict (he had secret stashes of candy in his clothing drawers), a heavy smoker, did cocaine every now and again, smoked pot, and ate way too much unhealthy food. I was an enabler and codependent, so this was perfect for me.

Ivan's father had just recently passed, and he was supposed to get some inheritance from him soon. He had to go to his father's apartment in the city and empty it out, clean it up, and get it ready to sell. I helped him. I had a van for my business, so of course that was used on several occasions to assist in the cleanup. He had three sisters, and a mother who was still alive. She was an addict, as well. She was very unhealthy and a heavy smoker. One of his sisters was gay, another was bisexual, and the third was deaf. All were strong willed and feisty. I began to see Ivan's patterns more and more. When you observe the family dynamics, you begin to unravel the story of a person and see how they became who they are now. His parents divorced when Ivan was a teenager. His father was a workaholic, which threw his mother into a deep depression. She attempted to commit suicide on several occasions. Ivan said that sometimes he would come home from school and find his mother unconscious from an overdose of sleeping pills. This happened far too often and eventually the father had enough and left. That left Ivan with three headstrong women and a sick mother. Do you think Ivan developed a bitter, unconscious resentment toward women? The baggage that we try to hide is like throwing a cloak over the elephant in the room. His was bursting with anger. He had diverticulitis and acid reflux disease, was on the verge of adult-onset diabetes, and God knows what other ailments were brewing inside him. Like my dad, all of his issues were trapped in his tissues.

How could I have been so naïve to all of this? Maybe because he was promising me a everything I had always wanted. So what if he wasn't the man I had envisioned? My mother gave him the thumbs up. She never liked Cooper, but she liked Ivan—only because he was Jewish. My mom had a thing for Jewish men. She thought they were all wonderful. People told me that Jewish men were good providers. What rubbish. Do not listen to people who speak of generalities. It doesn't matter if you're Jewish, Catholic, or whatever. If you're looking to get into a relationship only for monetary means, you will be disappointed. And the truth be told, that is exactly what I was looking for. I was getting tired of always being the breadwinner and I wanted someone to share the load. Oh, boy was I in for a rude awakening.

Things were happening so fast now. I had money saved to buy the house I was living in and I told Ivan that I had an opportunity to purchase it. He wanted to buy the house with me. I called the landlady, whom I had an excellent relationship with, and asked her how much she wanted for the house. She said that she would take $202,000. I had the money for the down payment. Ivan said that if I put down the money that he would pay me back half of it when his father's inheritance came through. Fair enough. We went through with the deal. His and my names were on the deed of the house. As I said, I always had a good eye for real estate and I knew this was a sweet deal. I wish I had a good eye for men, because I was heading into the fire with this guy.

Ivan quit or got laid off from his job in New Jersey and moved in with me. I'm not sure which one was the truth. He said he was burned out and wanted to do something else. Great, now I was the bread winner once again and I had three dependents. Because of all of this, my attitude was in the gutter, and everything around me was reflecting this.

# CHAPTER 19

Seeptember 11, 2001. What a beautiful day. I was just starting a new job at a client's home when I heard the news of the attack on the World Trade Center. I raced home. That was the beginning of so much tragedy for the world. A war was about to begin. On my home front, another kind of war was brewing. I took Naomi out of Catholic school because she continued to fail. I wasn't spending that kind of money to have her flunk. Back in public high school, she was repeating her behavior, only she was getting worse. She wasn't interested in going to school. She was staying out late without calling, and she was totally disrespecting me. I knew something was seriously wrong with the way she was acting but I didn't know what it was. I took her to see a psychologist. He worked out of his house, which was a total mess. I would think that a psychologist would have his act together and be organized. He was unhealthy, too. He didn't look good and he told me he was bordering on diabetes. Who was this guy? This was who my insurance company provided. He was basically useless. I had to do my own research to find out what Naomi was into. Money would suddenly disappear from my wallet. I thought I had more there than what was in it. I would begin to doubt myself. I thought maybe I was mistaken.

In the meantime, I would go to work, only to come home to Ivan, a fat slob watching TV. Not a welcoming site. There would be dirty dishes in the sink; I would think the least he could do was to clean them since he was home all day. He told me that I had two daughters who should be doing them. I was getting angrier by the day. I was at my wits end with the pressure of having one of my daughters mysteriously acting so differently and withdrawn from life, and a useless man, freeloading. I didn't know what to do.

I was looking for clues to Naomi's behavior problems, so I scoured her room from top to bottom. I found these empty, tiny little bags. They looked like marijuana bags, but something told me they weren't. They didn't have an odor, and there were a lot of them. That was all I found.

Confronting her was not getting me anywhere. I only heard lies. She had a boyfriend, Steve, who was also acting weird. I needed an answer fast and I got it. My intuition is so right on, and when I honor it, I will always find the answers.

I went for a walk, as I would mostly every night. On my walk, I found a needle. I thought it was odd to find one there. It gave me the creeps and I knew right then and there that I had my answer. I knew she had started to use heroin. My heart sank so deep that day. I went home and waited until Naomi came home. I asked her if I could see her arms. She was wearing long sleeves. She refused. I literally tackled her to the ground and pulled up her sleeves. Sure enough, I found track marks on her arms. That explained her peculiar behavior.

The first thing I did was call up her father. We needed to be on the same page and look for help. I had no idea what I was in for. This drug takes over your soul, your spirit, your body, and your mind. It is evil. It is like a black hole that sucks everything into its path of descruction. We found a place way upstate —a thirty-day rehab. That was all the insurance company offered, thirty days. We both drove her up there one icy-cold winter day. She was admitted, and we, the parents, were advised to seek counseling, too. They said that addiction is a family disease. I was willing and able to do whatever it took to help my daughter, who was only fifteen … my baby girl, whom I loved with all my heart. Edward was rather aloof and wasn't as devastated as I was. We drove back, together, and knew that she was in good hands. For the first time in a long time I felt peaceful.

Lilly knew what was going on but not to the full extent. I am sure she was hurting inside but did not let on to the fact. She never really rebelled. She always did well in school and never acted out beyond dying her hair different colors. One month it was shocking pink, then blue, blonde, and jet black. I didn't mind, and thought it was rather harmless. She did experiment with pot and cocaine, but I caught it right away, and it never became a problem. I was able to nip that in the bud immediately, thank God!

Naomi had a different personality. She was addictive by nature. I blamed myself for her addiction. This was my worst nightmare. How could this have happened? Was it the neighbors, April and Liz, who'd introduced this drug to her? Was it me who caused her to self-medicate? I also was dealing with embarrassment. We lived in a small community where everyone knew each other's business. The shame and the guilt were too much. I tortured myself. While I was able to gain some semblance of peace while Naomi was in rehab, thirty days came and went very fast … too fast. I was also very naïve to think that after thirty days Naomi would be cured of her addiction. Her boyfriend drove up with me to pick her up—mistake number one. Mistake number two was having her come home. She needed at least two years in some remote healing center to change her ways.

Her addiction escalated rapidly. Now checks were missing from my business account. Hundreds of dollars suddenly vanished.

It would be a few months before I was able to put a stop to this. I even went down to the police station and was going to have her arrested for doing this. It would have been a felony charge. But I just couldn't bring myself to press charges. When she lied to me, I became a raving lunatic. I was convinced that I could control her and stop this. I would follow her, take her to work with me, keep her under my watch as much as I could. But to little avail. This drug was way stronger and more powerful than my willpower.

On top of all this, Ivan said he was leaving. That actually was a good thing; however, he was suing me for half the house, since his name was on the deed. He'd had it all planned. He had all his things boxed up in the basement, where he had free storage until he was ready to pick it all up. He said he could not take the chaos anymore. I don't blame him. It was unbearable.

I remember him saying to me that he was going to force me to sell the house and give him half the money. Talk about kicking someone when they're down. I told him that I understood him wanting to leave; however, if it were me who was leaving, I would just walk away. I would never do that to anyone. He had finally found a woman he could pay back for all the crap he took from his mother and three sisters; and I was ripe for the taking.

Now I needed to find myself an attorney who would handle this. This is where the tides started to turn for me. I needed to get down on my knees and pray. I was so desperate for help. I found it in Al-Anon, a twelve-step program for people with loved ones who are addicts. I knew I was unable to cure this thing and that it had come from within Naomi. I didn't cause it, so I couldn't cure it, and I certainly couldn't control it, as they say in Al-Anon.

Naomi continued on her self-destructive rampage. A few arrests, impounding of cars, sleazy characters lurking around, and a few more stints in rehabs. I took her to conventional and unconventional treatments to help her get well. Nothing seemed to work. This forced me to take a good hard look at myself and my own addictions. I needed to begin to do the long hard road of healing myself. I was finally looking into all those deep dark places in me where I had stuffed all those unpleasant feelings from the past. They were all around me, anyway. Everywhere I turned, I was being confronted by some sort of conflict. My only refuge was work. How I held it all together, I really don't know. But that was about to take a landslide, too. There was no hiding place anymore. There was nowhere to stuff anything. It was full to the brim and leaking out.

# CHAPTER 20

My horticulture business was steady. I had made friends with a guy named Warren, who was also in the plant business, His son-in-law, Bob, would sometimes help me with some of my jobs. Bob was a godsend. He took over my accounts when I was unable to, and did a great job. People loved him; he was honest, meticulous, and smart. He also worked for Warren in his business.

Warren had another partner, Mark. Warren knew how hard working I was and how good I was with plants. He approached me to become partners with him, Mark and Bob. It sounded like a new folk group—Bob, Mark, Warren, and Karen. He explained to me that he was going to buy someone's business that was for sale and wanted me, to come into the deal. It sounded like a great idea. No red flags came up. No Jiminy Cricket on my shoulder warning me of any evil intentions. So I invested and we consummated the deal. We bought the accounts of this other guy's business, some equipment, and a van. The accounts were all outdoor installations. We would plant people's gardens and install pots with flowers. This kept us very busy from early May to the end of July. We were working seven days a week from morning to night, and it was brutal. I was exhausted.

Lilly was able to stay at her dad's while I was working and Naomi was doing her thing. My mind was always wondering where she was, who she was with, and what she was doing. I was obsessed with thinking about her. Finally, a dear friend, who was one of my angels, gave me a formula to relieve the heartache I was experiencing. She had a daughter who was a recovered heroin addict. She advised me to say "cancel, clear" every time I had a negative thought, and replace it with a positive one. She taught me another mantra: "Anything that is not for my highest good is uprooted, neutralized, and dissolved into the nothingness from where it came."

Sometimes I had to say these things thousands of times a day. Really, the negative thoughts were insidious. They would sneak in from every dark corner of my mind. But I was determined and persistent. I wasn't forcing or controlling my thoughts, either. When a negative thought came to me, I would say "cancel, clear" or the other phrase and replace it with something that felt better. Over and over and over again I had to do this until the pattern of thoughts became interrupted. Weeks went by before I got some relief from my own stinking thinking. Finally, I had a reprieve.

Besides being consistent with this formula, I also started journaling. I discovered *The Artist's Way* by Julia Cameron. It is sort of like a twelve-step program for artists or creative people—or really, anyone. The morning pages she recommended were such a huge help to rid myself of all the negativity trapped in my mind.

I thought that I had overcome my childhood wounds, but I was only bandaging them up by my next man or whatever else I used to relieve the pain I was feeling at the time. The morning pages gave me a way to release and look at the suffering I was stuffing deep inside of me for so many years. I was disciplined enough to follow through with getting up about 4:00 AM and writing three pages of whatever came out. No pre-thoughts, just pure "garbage out."

Another thing I did was read the Zohar. These are the sacred texts of the Kabbalah. After I wrote my three pages, I would read the Zohar for half an hour. I wanted to heal Naomi, my family, and myself. I was determined to find a way out of the hell I'd put myself and my family in. I created this mess and I knew I could create an alternate reality as well. All the books, tapes, and videos that I was devouring were fitting together like a puzzle. I knew that I was on the right path and that all the answers were inside of me. I knew that I needed to stay focused and persistent if I wanted to change.

When something manifests into physical form it is much more difficult to eradicate it from existence than when it is still in thought form. That is why it is so vital to be conscious of your thoughts. When you have a thought that is disempowering, you can "cancel, clear" it before you build on that thought and it starts to take form and root inside of your being. When you think this thought over and over again it will eventually seek expression through some practical means. The same is true for positive thoughts. Focus on what you want rather than what you don't want. This is the most difficult work. Harder than any physical labor, for sure.

I love James Allen's poem:

> *"Mind is the master power, that molds and makes. And man is mind, and the more he takes the tool of thought, and shapes it to his will, brings forth a thousand joys, or a thousand ills. He thinks in secret, and it comes to pass, environment is but his looking glass."*

Isn't that awesome? Really, that sums it all up. This is where I strayed and struggled all my life. My thoughts were leading me to dead ends and dark alleyways. I was finally seeing the connection between my thoughts, feelings, and actions. I was getting a glimpse into what my thinking was creating. But wait; I was not out of the woods yet. There were still more villains to overcome.

# CHAPTER 21

B ack on the horticulture trail, while work seemed to be never-ending, it did start to wane down around July and things began to settle back into a semi-normal schedule. Naomi moved out and was living with her new boyfriend, Justin. He was an addict, too, of course. Like attracts like. I was attending Al-Anon meetings regularly and still keeping my vigil with my morning pages, reading the Zohar, and praying everyday. The summer came and went.

Autumn arrived and the flower business picked up energy. It was fall planting time for Bulbs, Chrysanthemums, asters, and sedums. I was decorating with pumpkins, and planting cool-weather crops for our customers. I got through it without any major hiccups.

And then the storm approached. I didn't see this one coming. I hadn't seen any red flags, as I said. I was trying to reach Warren by phone to go over some work details and he wasn't returning my calls. I thought this was rather odd, so I called Bob to ask him if he'd heard from Warren. He said he would call him and get back to me. Well, he did get back to me with some very disturbing news. Warren told Bob to tell me that he was through with me. I was dismissed, discarded, and dispelled. But why? The first thing that ran through my mind was, "What did I do?"

Of course I thought it was me, that I'd done something wrong. Maybe I screwed up an account or something. But I didn't. I couldn't rationalize why Warren wanted me gone. Bob reassured me that I didn't do anything to cause this. He then told me that Warren's wife was jealous of my working with him and had given him an ultimatum. Either he stopped doing business with me, or she would leave him. Obviously he did not have the backbone to stand up to her and tell her that there wasn't anything going on between us, which there wasn't, and that it was strictly a business arrangement. The last thing on my mind was having an affair with him. Especially after working twelve-hour days, dealing with a man who was suing me, saving one daughter from a life of addiction, raising another, and trying to find my serenity. You have got to be kidding me—really? I was in shock, disbelief, and I was so confused. I needed to hear from Warren himself to see if this was true. He finally called me and said straight out he wanted nothing to do with me ever again, that I should never speak, call, or have any contact with him.

This really stung. I had put so much blood, sweat, and tears into this business and for him to cut me off with such a cold tongue really hurt me to the core.

I could have become bitter and angry toward life, but I choose to rise above. I did play the victim for a while. I allowed myself to mourn and grieve over this, but I had been working too hard on my peace of mind to allow this to ruin it for me. Naomi and Lilly were the most important gifts in my life and I knew I needed to stay strong for them.

I was able to get my investment back by retaining an attorney to sue them for defamation of character and punitive damages for him not wanting me in the business. If I wanted to play hardball, I could have gone for the jugular and really sued the crap out of him, but I just wanted to walk away. I wanted to put this behind me and focus on what was important in my life. He did return my investment, and I still had my own business, which I had maintained while in this partnership. But I never felt the same about it ever again. I was still licking my wounds while I continued my work, and it took its toll on me. I was losing accounts and not caring any more. Though I continued to love working with plants and all that nature had to offer, I wanted out of the horticultural business.

My passion drifted toward natural health, the spirit world, and subjects regarding the mind and how to tap into unseen powers. Horticulture was still a big part of all this, but I just didn't want to do it as a business anymore. I felt there was something bigger calling me.

Then I discovered coaching. I saw the movie *The Secret*, and knew it was exactly what direction my life was heading toward. I finally understood the connection between my thoughts, feelings, and actions. I'd taken a course through the Napoleon Hill Foundation. Napoleon Hill wrote books, gave lectures and developed audio and video programs on personal development. He wrote the book Think and Grow Rich in 1937. (I wish my parents had the awareness to discover this book.)I was so thirsty for this knowledge. I was a voracious reader of any book or subject dealing with the mind and metaphysics. Through my studies of natural health, and understanding the power of thought, I was integrating all this knowledge into my soul and awakening my mind, body, and spirit. Books by Emmet Fox, Gary Zukav, Louise Hay, and Thomas Troward were just a few of the authors I read and studied. I believe in spontaneous healing, and I knew that my life would be changed if I began focusing on what I wanted rather than on what wasn't working—which had been my pattern from the time I was in my mother's womb. The pattern had become so ingrained within me that I needed to be diligent if I wanted things to improve.

Through my morning pages, spiritual reading, prayer, and meditation, things were slowly improving. Consciously, I was willing myself to believe this. But it is in the subconscious where the changes really need to start. I was fooling myself. You see, your conscious and subconscious mind need to be in harmony. If there is any ambiguity, the old patterns will win and no real change will ever occur. I was now taking three steps forward and two steps back, so there was some improvement. I knew I had to be patient. It was like cleaning up a polluted lake. Every day small efforts will eventually result in a significant change.

───────※───────

I sold my business, my BMW, and buckled down on my next chapter: life coaching. I invested tens of thousands of dollars on my education in this field, and I still am so happy and grateful that I did. The knowledge and education I received was priceless. I am still investing and continue to learn. Through all the wisdom and truth I sought and found, patterns still run deep. At any moment if I took my eye off my goal, wham, back I went into the prison of my mind. Back to the old pattern.

Around this time I bumped into Cooper. I was given another test to see if I was really mastering what I was learning. Oh, how good it was to see a familiar face. I still longed for a relationship and I convinced myself and him that we should try again. That I'd made a big mistake, and we were really meant for one another. My brain's wiring went completely bunkers. The neurons, axons, and dendrites were all malfunctioning. What was I thinking? I wasn't; that's the thing. My hormones were addicted to men. I was an addict who'd come across her drug of choice, and I relapsed again.

They say relapse is a part of recovery. Yes, it is. I had him move back in with me. At least this time I was able to see rather quickly that it was never going to work. In the time we were apart, I had traveled light years, while Cooper was the same man he always was. Not that there was anything wrong with where he was mentally, but I knew I couldn't go back there. So I had to tell him I'd made a mistake. He was pissed, rightfully so, but left rather quickly. This time at least he didn't ask for any money. I didn't have any to give.

So onward and upward I went. I am a rescuer by nature; this is one of my strong archetypes. Life is full of tests and trials. Just when you think you have learned your lesson, a little fire gets thrown your way to see if you can handle it.

---

At about the same time, my mom was struggling with the house my brother and I had grown up in. She was having trouble with the tenants. There were more and more storms, some of them hurricanes, that were affecting the house and she was pressing the panic button. I would get frequent frantic calls from her about how she couldn't deal with all the problems that come along with an older home.

My brother thought that it would be a good time for her to sell. I agreed. I had wanted my mom to sell that house a long time ago and had been pressing her every year to do so, but she wanted no part in hearing this. She got angry every time I brought it up. But now that my brother was on board, she was ready. The challenge was, where would she go? Here is where my rescuing archetype kicked in. I could have her live with me. Through all my newly learned thought patterns, I thought I would be able to heal our relationship, which had been strained for years. Yes—we could bond and find some common ground.

You see, the problem was that all my negative thoughts had originated from my parents. This is where I'd learned all the behaviors that weren't working. So why would I put her directly under my roof? Good question. I wanted to get away from all of this. I tried hard to push all the negativity away. (What you resist will persist.) Whatever I tried to forcefully push away, came back in an even bigger way. The lesson here is not to push it away, but rather accept that the negativity came from my parents, and come to terms with it. Big lesson.

———— ᴍᴏᴏᴇᴛᴏᴏᴛᴏᴏᴏᴍ ————

Lilly was getting ready for college. She was heading off to Colorado. She always knew what she wanted and went for it. God bless her. At least I was able to transmute these positive thoughts into her mind. She was always an excellent student and if that was where she wanted to go, I was all for it. Through my business's income, some grants, and loans, we were able to swing it. It was a private school, so it did cost quite a bit, along the lines of $55,000 a year. Ouch! We are still paying off those student loans. Lilly and I scouted out schools there for two years in a row to make sure that was really where she wanted to be. It was a beautiful place, and she loved it there.

So while I was helping her prepare for her first year of school, buying her all the things she would need, my mom was putting her house up for sale.

Before Lilly's move to Colorado, I had rescued a dog from the shelter, a pit bull mix that I named Kismet. He was very abused and afraid of his own shadow. The attorney who was handling my case with Ivan had said to me, "If you want to rescue someone again, rescue a dog instead." Good advice—and I took it.

Unfortunately, Kismet started to get sick. I didn't know what was wrong with him. I thought he may have been jealous of the attention another little dog was getting. That other little dog was Shadow, a little runt of a dog that Naomi had bought from a breeder. He was a long-hair Chihuahua that had mange. Since Naomi seemed to be doing OK, I had her move back in with me after she had a fight with her boyfriend. Big mistake, but I still needed to learn this. Anyway, I didn't want this little rodent of a dog. I told her to get rid of it. I didn't even want to look at him. The only reason I didn't want to look at him was because I know I'm really a softy and that I would wind up loving him—which I did.

Kismet was starting to lose weight, so I took him to the vet. After a full examination, they discovered that he had advanced kidney disease. They said he must have had Lyme disease that was never diagnosed, which resulted in his kidneys failing. Eighty percent of his kidneys were not functioning. The only humane thing to do was to put him to sleep. Lilly came with me to do this and we both were devastated.

Two days later, I was flying out to Colorado with her to set her up at the university dormitories. My little girl was going to be so far away from home. I had some growing up to do, myself.

I remember the plane ride home. So many thoughts were running through my mind. Thank God for my new spiritual understanding. I was able to be at peace with it all. I had Naomi and little Shadow with me, but Naomi was still creating way too much drama. I didn't want to be a part of it, so I asked her to leave. That was, by far, the most difficult decision I had to make in my life. I knew I had to trust in the universe enough to let her go. She was the beautiful child I'd given birth to; however, she was God's child, too, and she was in God's hands.

It was also the best decision I made, for her as well as for me. She moved to Newark, New Jersey, one of the toughest neighborhoods in that area, with her girlfriend Beth. She'd always worked, so she was able to support herself. That was another thing that she learned from me: my strong work ethic. Her little doggie, Shadow, went with her.

I was alone and feeling that rescuing urge coming on again. I certainly wasn't looking for a man, but I'd grown attached to that little runt of a dog. I convinced Naomi that Shadow needed to be with me. That she was working long hours and I had more time to care for him. This was true, although it was a ploy to snatch him away so I would have something to nurture.

I still have that little doggie and he has grown into the most adorable dog in the world, with an amazing personality. Naomi claims to this day that I kidnapped her dog. I guess I did, but I justified it by telling myself that I was better able to care for him. That was my rationale. Sometimes I think we "ration-lies" to convince ourselves of something that may not be true at all.

And so I was living alone with little Shadow for a short time before my mom moved in. I didn't hire movers, and I didn't want my mom doing any heavy lifting, so I single-handedly moved her into my home. I must have made dozens of trips back and forth moving all of her things. She sold most of the furniture, but boy, did she accumulate things over the years—boxes' and boxes' worth.

At first, I thought it was going to be a good thing, that she would really like it here. After all, it is so peaceful. But she had a hard time adjusting to the quiet. She needed drama, noise, and activity to keep away the noise inside her head. She complained constantly. She was bored; she couldn't get to a store since she didn't drive anymore; and on and on. I would suggest she join the senior organization, but she always had some excuse as to why she couldn't. Her negativity was really jarring.

I needed to find some work, since money was getting tight again, so I got a job working for a chiropractor in town. I knew working with people in the health field would be good training for me. I really enjoyed it; however, it wasn't enough pay to support my needs. I found another job working for a Nursery. I was back in the horticultural world, although this time I was employed rather than being the employer. I was working six days a week and long hours. I knew the business and that was part of the deal. We had many celebrities come into the place, since it was the most recognized nursery in town. I was able to earn commissions on my sales and over time I earned a good salary.

Right as I was starting this job in May, I finally settled my case with Ivan. I had to pay him $55,000 and attorney fees of about $7,000. Ouch! That hurt. At least it was settled and done with. I was free to move forward with my life. This entanglement had held me back from doing anything with the house until it was cleared. Now that it was over, I was able to remortgage the house for $300,000, pay Ivan and my attorney, and have some left over for home improvements.

My mom had money from the sale of her house, so she too invested in renovating the house. We opened up the wall between the kitchen and the living room, put in new windows and new wood floors, and finished the basement. It came out gorgeous. It was great timing, since I was at work all day while men worked on the home. It kept my mom occupied as well. She liked when there were people around and that is what she got for the summer. Lilly, too, was home for the summer, but she was independent and doing her own thing. She was working at a marina about twenty minutes away. Her father and I bought her an old BMW to get around in. The summer came and went. Lilly was back off to college and doing magnificently. Every semester she made the dean's list. Naomi was still in Newark, my mom was settling in a bit better, and I was finishing up work at the nursery. Most of the local workers would get laid off for the winter and collect unemployment until the spring starts up again. I never collected this before and thought it rather interesting. It is nice to get money for doing nothing. I know that, as a tax-payers, we pay into the system, but I still found it difficult to comprehend. For the first time in my life, I was collecting unemployment. I received about $325.00 a week, which was about a quarter of what I earned when I worked, but it was free money. The thing about unemployment, disability, and welfare, is that you can get a bit too comfortable in the system and then find it difficult to get out. There are those who really need the help, but I know so many people who have become dependent on these programs. It becomes a crutch that weakens the spirit, soul, and mind.

———⟶⟵———

I wanted to start my coaching business, so I reached out to find ways to accomplish this. At the same time I saw an ad in the local paper for a health and wellness company that sounded right along the lines of what I was interested in, so I called. The woman on the phone told me that they were having a presentation at someone's home, so I went. It was about customized vitamins and other supplements for optimum health. There were six different in-home tests that you could take to see where your markers were for adrenaline function, estrogen levels, food allergies, and a few other tests. I thought it was a brilliant idea. The lab they were using was one of the best in the country, too. I signed on board to distribute them. It was a multilevel marketing company, which I wasn't familiar with at first, but since I had time on my hands, I started learning about it. The company was called Optimum Health at the time. What I liked about this business was that they encouraged people in personal growth. I was attracted to the people in the company, so I became more and more involved with the business.

I also was beginning to offer classes at our local library on various topics focused around the idea of personal development. I opened an LLC that I called Mind Power. Since this is what I was striving for all my life, I thought it was an appropriate name for my new business.

We teach what we need to learn the most and that is exactly what I was doing. I loved teaching, coaching, and speaking about the power of our minds. The passion I have for this is right up there with dancing and horticulture. Actually, I feel they are all related. Since order is the first law of the universe, and everything in nature is in perfect order, I felt that this suited me to want to coach. The second law of the universe is movement. We live in an ocean of motion. Everything is in constant movement at all times.

That is why I love dance. I love the orderly movement of my body. When our conscious and subconscious minds are in harmony, our cells, organs, and systems all move together in perfect health. However, when they are not, that is when disease occurs. I desired to help people understand these laws and principles so that they could begin to live in ease rather than create an unhealthy body. I knew that this is how people begin to get sick.

A gentleman who lived in my small town was involved with putting shows on the local cable TV channel. We spoke and he wanted to air a program on the mind power. Wow—I would be on television. Although it seemed like a big deal, I would always forget to let people know about it. I taped a show every week, and it aired twice a week. It was really thought-provoking. I never let my ego get big over this. I had my email showing on the screen and received a few responses. A few people would recognize me from the show and tell me how much they enjoyed it, but I never got any business from it.

Money was getting tighter and tighter. I was starting to get worried about that. What I was teaching—about staying positive and keeping your thoughts focused on what you want and off of what you don't want—was hitting all too close to home. It is challenging to do this when you're seeing your checking account get lower and lower. I didn't like it, and I was borrowing money from my mother now. A few reflexology clients came to my home for treatment, but that wasn't enough to pay the bills. My coaching business and the supplement marketing business were not taking off yet. More and more money was going out and less and less was coming in.

Then I landed a speaking engagement at a nearby insurance agency to motivate their staff, which I was thrilled about. My presentation required a projector, and I needed a small card table for this but didn't want to spend a lot of money buying a new one. I went to a thrift shop that a friend of mine owned, where I thought I would be able to pick one up for a good price. Lo and behold, while I was there I encountered a man who was working there. Now my guard was down. That was a mistake. I always need to have my radar on alert when it comes to men, since they are my Achilles heel. His name was William; Bill for short. He came across as a fit, good-looking, attentive man. He was showing me some tables that didn't work for me, and somehow we got into the conversation of nutrition. I gave him my spiel about the network marketing company I was involved with. We all thought we were going to make millions, but it only came crashing down on us instead.

Anyway, he seemed interested and wanted to know more. I invited him to a presentation. I told him that I would pick him up. He agreed. Now I really had no intentions of getting involved with him; however, he had different thoughts. He thought I was a hot mama, which I am, from a man's point of view.

I picked him up at his place. He was renting a room in a house with other tenants—red flag number one. He didn't drive—red flag number two. He didn't own a credit card—red flag number three. I must have completely fallen asleep at the wheel, or he'd hypnotized me. We went to the presentation, which was uplifting. He said he loved the product and thought it was a great idea. He wanted to join. Great! My first "down line." (Down line are people you sign into your business and you earn a commission on.) The only trouble was, he didn't have a credit card. He had cash, so I got the brilliant idea of putting it on my card as long as he gave me the money. This was really poor judgment on my part, but I just wanted to help him and I wanted to build a client base. The warning signs were all over the place; Jimmy Cricket was going crazy on my shoulder, trying to warn me that this guy was bad news. But no, I went down the rabbit hole ... I allowed him to enter my life.

At first it seemed like it would be wonderful. Again, beware of wolves disguised in sheep's clothing. He was a raging alcoholic. And I mean raging. I never met anyone who drank and got as completely comatose as him. He was on social services and I came to realize that he was a very sick man. Nevertheless I had him move in with me. This was a manifestation of my control tendencies and my rescuing archetype.

Right after New Year's, 2009, I broke my arm walking on the beach. It was a bitter cold day and I was running backward, playing with Shadow. Bill was with me; he took me to the hospital, where they gave me some pain pills and wrapped my arm up until I could get it operated on. That same evening, Bill decided to go on a binge, the likes of which I have never seen. That night was the first time I had to call the police on him.

After the third time of him being in drunken stupor and my having to call the police, I changed the locks to my home and was done with him. I couldn't believe I'd actually done it again. Like a true addict, I too had sunk deeper and deeper into my addiction and had relapsed again.

This time I hit bottom. Through his dysfunction, he'd cured me. Although it was so disturbing and so completely crazy, I finally got it. I had to stop! That was it—I was over and done with the drama of men. I had learned my lesson.

The people who press our buttons can be our greatest teachers. He was a master. Don't ever shoot the messenger. He sent me a special delivery alright: Stay awake, stay alert, and observe the patterns. He was another stray I thought I could fix, super-size, clean up, and improve. Instead of staying focused on my own course, I drifted into the arms of a strange man looking for daddy dearest to cure my ills; but it doesn't work like that. The path of least resistance was the path toward a life of misery.

I had such bad vibes from Bill that I didn't even want to live in my own home anymore. It was disturbing to know that this man was sleeping in my bed, sitting on my couch, and hanging out in my kitchen. Anywhere I went in my home, I felt his presence still lingering. I wanted to get a fresh start. Besides, I was in such debt that the best thing for me to do was to sell my home. I needed a change. My mom and I were not getting along, which was added pressure. So much for Mind Power. I was helping others and here I was with all this trauma. I was the classic "wounded healer," another archetype that Carl Jung had written about: I was helping other people find clarity and peace of mind, while I was still in need of it myself.

There are two ways to change a pattern. One is through shock, and that is what, through Bill, finally happened to me with men. Bill helped me see that I was finished with dysfunctional relationships. This way is really not that advisable because of the strain it puts on your nervous system. The second is spaced repetition—doing something over and over and over again; this is how we learn almost everything. Good and bad habits are formed this way. No pill is going to cure your ills, only persistent effort.

# CHAPTER 22

After all these traumatic years, my dear grandma Amo had passed. She lived to the ripe old age of ninety-nine. Pat, my girls' grandmother, died several years before. My precious Nadia had left this plane, as well as some other very dear friends. Naomi's boyfriend, Justin, and another friend's son died before their time, because of addiction. And life went on.

These were more lessons to be learned. Life is for expansion and fuller expression. It is always moving toward the future, but not without its growing pains and its fair share of loss. What I have learned is that the more I focus on the present moment and finding my bliss now, the more I am creating a fulfilling future and healing my past.

I am rewriting the story, and I believe it is never too late to have a happy childhood. The past is history, the future is a mystery, but right now is a gift, and that's why they call it the present. There are no gift receipts; no refunds, no exchanges, and it is never given twice. We must open our present right now; and when we do, we will discover our purpose, our truth, and our bliss. It is possible. I know; I have been there. There are no accidents. There are no coincidences. And don't be afraid to put your life out there on the edge. You never know what will come back to you if you give life your best—you're whole self.

# Chapter 23

Although it was one of the hardest decisions I ever had to make, I put my house up for sale. Homes can be such emotional soft spots for most people, and mine certainly was for me. I had raised my children in this house. This was the place where I'd started over by myself, a place I'd given so much love and energy to … but it was time to move on to the next chapter of my life.

I needed a whole new perspective. It was a beautiful home in a much-desired location. Although the market wasn't anywhere near its peak, I knew I would be able to get a good price for it. I had many lookers and a few interested parties who offered me some lowball prices. I refused to take anything but the asking price. I knew I'd priced it fairly.

Then along came a couple who really loved it. At first they too offered less than what I wanted, but then they came back with the full price. They paid in cash, so it made the transaction very easy.

It felt so good to know that I was on to my next adventure. It was such a liberating feeling to be able to create something entirely new in my life. I had two months to find a place to call my new home and set my mom up in a place as well. I had a newfound girlfriend through the network marketing company who wanted me to move closer to the city, where she was living.

Since I'd grown up in the next town over, my mother and I were very familiar with the location.

I thought it would be a good move for her since she knew the area, and for me since it was a vibrant town. Pamela, my friend, was having some money issues and wanted me to help her out. I'd already loaned her a few hundred dollars for a new cell phone. Now she asked if we could move in together. The rents were rather steep and I thought finding a place to share might be a good idea to save some money. I scouted out a few homes with a realtor and found a nice place. It had a new kitchen, a huge living room and a dining room, too. That was going to be our new pad. The thing was, Pamela didn't have any money. We needed to put down a security deposit and one month's rent, plus the real estate fees. She didn't have the cash so I was the one who laid out the payments. She was going to pay me back in monthly installments. I have got to be the most trusting person in the world ... or the stupidest. I like to think of myself as trusting.

We both had intentions on building our network marketing business together, while having the occasional girls' night out and enjoying being near the beach. She knew I had three cats and my little dog Shadow. She had a little dog of her own. When we moved in together, she had no furniture and I had extra, so I loaned her some for her space.

I was looking to get a job right away to pay for my living expenses, since I didn't want to tap into the money I'd made on the sale of the house. Another friend mentioned to me that the Mystic Luncheonette was looking for a waitress. It was only two blocks away, so I went in to ask if they needed any help. One of the owners, Ralph, said yes, they were looking for someone, and if I wanted to come in next week to train that would be great.

Herein lies the beginning of my position as a server again. I had come full circle. I started working there in September of 2011. I hadn't waitressed for some time, and in a fast-paced luncheonette, I was off my game.

I was so nervous when I started. It seemed like I made millions of mistakes. The computer program alone was so new to me. I think they were ready to fire me because I was so bad. The short-order cooks who work there are short tempered, too. They let you know in not-too-kind words if you mess up on any orders. The feeling of not being good enough resurfaced. It seemed to be coming up through my pores and oozing out of my skin.

When you begin something new, you're not always good at it. As a matter of fact, you can be downright awful at it, but if you want to get better at it you must break through that terror barrier and persist. Action conquers fear. I would go back home to the apartment and lick my wounds, knowing I was still a good person.

The people that work there tend to be a bit rough around the edges. There is a lot of screaming, yelling, verbal abuse, joking, gossip, and sexual innuendo. A huge part of me felt that I was too sensitive for this line of work. I would have nightmares of being yelled at by one of the girls behind the counter. When I told her about it, she laughed so hard; there was no compassion at all. Could I survive working there? Many of the other servers were very nice, and helped me out as best they could. Little by little, I got into the groove of things. It took me a long time, but now I'm comfortable at handling the speed and flow that is necessary in this place.

After less than a year of living with Pamela, we both wanted out. Thank God. The landlords approached us and asked if we wanted to terminate our lease. They wanted us out, too. They liked me but did not like Pamela. She brought in bedbugs and blamed it on the apartment. It was disgusting. We went to small claims court, trying to have the landlords pay for the exterminator. We lost. Somehow Pamela convinced me that they were there when we moved in. She moved in two months before me, and was always complaining about being bit. Since it was summer, I thought it must have been mosquitoes. Bedbugs never even crossed my mind. We eventually called an exterminator, who cleaned the apartment. That was one of the many incidents I had with her. She was a master manipulator and I am a classic pleaser. (Another of my archetypes) By May, I'd found a house twenty minutes away and she found an apartment in town, which her son cosigned with her.

━━━∿◦◦◦◦◦∿━━━

I was so happy to have my own place. The small house I moved into was perfect for me and my animals. I loved living alone. I have no problem enjoying my own company. I can sing and dance to my heart's desire, which I often do. I have come a long way from where I began. I still have to be aware of who I allow into my life, but I am not interested in rescuing anyone anymore. I have put my full attention on helping people be honest, rescue themselves and discovering their truth.

I have traveled to many places, but the deepest one was within. It was there that I unearthed treasures, gifts, and talents far beyond anything I thought possible at one time. Twenty years ago, I would have never gotten in front of a large audience to speak. Now I am confident and immensely enjoy speaking. I feel comfortable in my own skin. My last big trip was to Pucallpa, Peru, where I traveled alone into the Amazon. There I met with a shaman and participated in ayahuasca ceremonies. Ayahuasca is a naturally abundant vine in the forest that when harvested, puts you in an altered state of consciousness. Most people thought I was crazy. They were worried for me and thought that I was venturing out too far, but I wanted to experience this.

It was scary, yet fascinating. I was able to access the deepest parts of my subconscious mind, all the fear that was locked deep in my cellular memory. I wanted to face my fears head-on, and I did. I gained awareness about things I've never had before. Something shifted inside me. Something no one and nothing can take away. It gave me true knowledge of who I am. There is a calmness that rests over me now. My aura has shifted and I am committed to my pursuits in life coaching and being a Nia dance instructor (Nia combines yoga with modern dance and martial arts). I have found my bliss. My passion for these things is stronger than ever. I read something spiritual every day, and practice what I preach. I have fun, I laugh a lot, and I stay disciplined to my practice. I always want to learn, grow, and become more of who I am. I am so grateful for my journey, which has shown me the path of freedom, I no longer bear the chains of the negativity that only served to drag me down.

The greatest gift we humans have been given is the freedom to choose. We can choose any thought we want and believe anything we want. If we don't like our circumstance or the condition we are in, we can choose differently. If we really grasp this notion, we can set ourselves free.

I choose to serve. *"Everybody can be great, because anybody can serve. You don't have to have a college degree to serve. You don't have to make your subject and verb agree to serve. You only need a heart full of grace. A soul generated by love."*—Martin Luther King, Jr. *"Only a life lived in service of others is worth living."*—Albert Einstein. These are my two favorite quotes on serving. So I choose to serve and waitress for right now. When the time is right, I will move on. But for now, I am exactly where I need to be.

I have the privilege of sharing my knowledge with anyone who is open to listen. I am in front of souls who are traveling on this earth with me. We are all spiritual beings having a human experience, whether we know it or not. How we choose to live our human experience is a personal journey. We come into this world on our own, and will leave it the same way. So the more you get to know yourself and fully love yourself, the more at peace you will be. The more you understand yourself, the more you will know others. We all have tremendous power within us. When we focus our thoughts on the things we desire, we can attract anything into our lives.

There is a wonderful book entitled *Your Invisible Power,* written by Genevieve Behrend back in the early 1900s. There is a quote from the book I have memorized, and I repeat it often: *"When your understanding grasps the power to visualize your heart's desire and hold it with your will, you will begin to attract all things necessary for the fulfillment of that picture, through the harmonious vibrations of the law of attraction."* You see, everything vibrates. Everything has a frequency. The more you are in harmony with what it is you want, the more you will attract it in your life. But you must also take action and you must follow your intuition. There is no attraction without the action. Merely dreaming of a thing is the first step, now you have to take another and then another and you will then step into that thing that was once your fantasy. Never give up. It might take days, weeks, or even years for it to come into fruition, but when the time is right, it will come.

The laws of nature are constantly working. They work for everybody, every time, every where. They are working for me at the luncheonette, where I serve people every day. I know I am here for a reason. I know God has put me here to learn lessons and to help others. I fully accept this and serve with gratitude. There are some people who are difficult to please, and I have learned to understand that not everyone is ready to be awakened to their higher self. But I have also learned that most people are good. If you find an opening in their heart, you can disarm just about anyone.

I get to have in-depth talks with a rabbi who comes in for breakfast. I get to work on solving the Jumble and Cryptoquote from *Newsday* with the two Bills who come in almost every morning. Sometimes, I help out struggling young women who are trying to get clean and sober. They tell me they are new to the program of AA, and I talk with them and sometimes buy them breakfast. I'm not in AA, but I continue to follow the Al-Anon principles and know the Twelve Steps. I reach out and help those in need.

I am not bitter, angry, or resentful about any of my past relationships. We are all doing the best we can with the awareness we have at the moment. I wish my exes well and have forgiven them, as I hope they have all forgiven me of my sins. I'm far from perfect, and I continue to learn new lessons every day.

I never want to stop learning. I stay thirsty and hungry for new experiences, knowledge, and wisdom. Every day is an opportunity to be better than the day before, to step out of my comfort zone, and to grow.

# EPILOGUE

I have come a long way from the insecure and frightened young girl who was looking for love in all the wrong places. I am now confident, happy, and free to choose anything I want, and for right now, I have chosen to work at the Mystic Luncheonette as a server.

We are all servers, in one way or another. Whether you are a sales person, a clergy man, a parent, an office worker, or a CEO, we are all serving one another.

The question is, are we doing our best work? Do we have compassion for one another? Give your best and you will receive even more. You reap what you sow. Just like in gardening, you must plant the seeds in the spring in order to harvest their abundance in the fall.

I have been so blessed to have had all the trials and tribulations in my life, as they've molded me into who I am today. I wouldn't change a thing. It has all been for a reason and for my highest good. I know this now. The greatest journey is the one you take within to truly know yourself.

I am a spiritual waitress, having anything but an ordinary life. I continue to empower people through motivational and inspirational talks, coaching private clients, dancing, staying curious about everything, and loving people, animals, nature, and all of life. I practice what I preach and walk the talk, and I am learning not to take myself too seriously anymore. We are all walking the path of enlightenment at different stages. It doesn't matter how or what you are serving, all that matters is that you give from an open heart.

I am serving soul food—food for your soul. When I deliver your eggs, pancakes, or sandwiches, know that I am a light worker. My DNA is changing from carbon to crystalline based. I am here to serve humanity and send a message of love and light. I still ask God every morning, "How may I serve?" And every night I ask again, "Dear God, how may I serve to my highest calling?"

My answer is: "As you are. Keep on serving!"

And so I shall.

# The End

CPSIA information can be obtained at www.ICGtesting.com
Printed in the USA
LVOW08s0011260714

396050LV00002B/3/P